Princeton Theological Monograph Series

Dikran Y. Hadidian

General Editor

39

THE LOSS AND RECOVERY OF
TRANSCENDENCE

The Will to Power and the Light of Heaven

THE LOSS
and
RECOVERY
of
TRANSCENDENCE

THE WILL TO POWER AND THE LIGHT OF HEAVEN

John C. Robertson, Jr.

PICKWICK PUBLICATIONS
ALLISON PARK, PENNSYLVANIA

Copyright © 1995 by John C. Robertson

Published by

Pickwick Publications
4137 Timberlane Drive
Allison Park, PA 15101-2932
USA

Printed on Acid Free Paper in the United States of America

Library of Congress Cataloging-in-Publication Data

Robertson, John C.
    The Loss and Recovery of Transcendence : the will to power and the light of heaven / John C. Robertson, Jr.
        p. cm. -- (Princeton theological monograph series ; 39)
    Includes bibliographical references.
    ISBN 1-55635-027-9
    1. Transcendence of God. 2. Technology--Religious aspects--Christianity. 3. Civilization, Modern--20th century. 4. Presence of God.   I. Title. II. Series.
    BT124.5.R63   1995
    231' .4--dc20   95-5874
                                                                          CIP

To

Joan, Eric, and Mark

"Where I found the living, there I found will to power; and even in the will of those who serve I found the will to be master."

Friedrich Nietsche
Thus Spoke Zarathustra

"In our age, the I-It relation, gigantically swollen, has usurped, practically uncontested, the mastery and the rule. The I of this relation, as I that possesses all, makes all, succeeds with all, this I that is unable to say Thou, unable to meet a being essentially, is the lord of the hour. This self-hood that has become omnipotent, with all the It around it, can naturally acknowledge neither God nor any genuine absolute which manifests itself to [us] as of non-human origin. It steps in between and shuts out from us the light of heaven."

Martin Buber
The Eclipse of God

CONTENTS

ix

PREFACE

What is it about the modern western phase of human history that has caused a sense of the presence of God to grow so dim? Some sense of the Divine Transcendent has accompanied, nourished, and challenged almost every historical period and society of which we have record. A mutation is occurring, however, in the modern West. C.S. Lewis refers to the unchristening of European literature in the last two centuries.[1] Pitirim Sorokin observes that whereas in the high Middle Ages 97% of the subjects in the fine arts had to do with religious motifs and only 3% depicted secular life, today the ratio has been almost exactly inverted.[2]

According to a recent census of the world's religions, moreover, modern Westerners are giving up the practice of their religions at the rate of some 7,600 per day (while at least Christianity and Islam continue to increase in number in other parts of the world, Africa for example.)[3] So we ask: What is it about the modern Western situation that is causing the experience of God to grow dim for so many in the Western world?

Of course, one must not exaggerate. There are individuals among us for whom God is quite immediate. It is true, furthermore, that there have always been sceptics and atheists. One of the distinctive qualities of our situation, however, is that it is not just that the affirmation of God is being denied, but the very question of God has become *unreal* for perhaps a majority. And though there are striking outbreaks of collective religious enthusiasm from time to time, which may bear promise, they are all too often characterized by subjectivism, group egotism, and intellectual primitivism and are in the service of a reactionary social agenda of one sort or another. Classical religion is, in any case, decreasingly a determining factor in our public life. Surely, Nietzsche's well-known story of the madman has become a parable of our time. His deep felt cry for God, you will recall, was hardly intelligible to the noonday crowd in the marketplace. It was met with puzzlement and dismissive laughter.

That something of importance and not yet fully understood has occurred in Western history is clear. There has been a "collision" between the classical traditions and modern sensibilities, is one way of describing it.[4] Nietzsche spoke even more dramatically of the "death of God." And Martin Buber spoke, only a bit less extremely, of the "eclipse of God."Whatever the gains and losses of the new situation, it is clear that a mutation or major adjustment in our tradition(s) is a hallmark of the modern age. It has been an unsettling time for religion, and since religion has long been at the heart of our civilization, the fate of religion could hardly be of more importance for our culture at large. That the new situation has been some time in the making and is still with us (whatever the vagaries of journalistic opinion) is clear. What its causes and meanings are, however, is far from clear. Hence what follows is somewhat tentative. It is a groping attempt to identify and comprehend two of the most dominant strands of our cultural life and to attend to the fate of the key question of religion, the question of God, in each, with a view to understanding better our present spiritual situation.

Because I am trying to grasp large and dynamic cultural and intellectual trends and movements, I mention many names, but the contours of my findings and the chain of my argument can be fairly clearly delineated as follows.

The first chapter deals with what I have called scientific objectivism, a way of thinking embraced by (and embracing) not only many scientists and philosophical positivists but also, albeit in a less explicit and systematic way, a large number of the rest of the population. What all have in common is the conviction that the scientific method or something like it is the best access we have to truth and that, since belief in God is unconvincing as a scientific hypothesis, it is untenable. However, the innocence, neutrality, and adequacy of this method are called in question.

The second chapter deals with humanistic or emancipatory subjectivism. Its problem with belief in God is less that it is judged to be cognitively dubious than that it is deeply felt to be morally oppressive. Among the many notable representatives of this way of thinking, e.g., Feuerbach, Marx, Freud, Sartre, and Daly, I focus on Nietzsche, because of his influence and the acuity of his observations and criticisms. While humanistic subjectivism provides a much needed purification of religion, the vision of unqualified self-creation, self-legislation, autonomy, will to power, etc., is questioned.

The third chapter identifies and discusses a remarkable parallel between recent English speaking philosophy of science and Heideggerian intellectual history. Both expose the role of interests in human knowledge, more specifically in scientific enquiry and its method. Kuhn discovers the role of paradigms that are historically constructed and politically negotiated. Hesse speaks of the role of self-understanding in investigation. Heidegger argues that the interest informing distinctively modern science is a technological interest, the desire to control, manage, and dominate. This prompts Heidegger to challenge the usual account of modern technology as the application of science to practical problems: to the contrary, modern science was constituted from the outset by this interest. This also prompts Heidegger to posit an inner affinity between modern science and technology on the one hand and the Nietzschean will to power on the other. Hence I argue that there is an inner affinity between the objectivism of the first chapter and the subjectivism of the second: both are rooted in a common orientation or way of being-in-the-world, a technological way. There is no need to demonize this technological mentality, for its benefits are obvious, e.g., in health care and food production and distribution. However, taken alone, it shuts down our access to the Transcendent. Can we have technology and Transcendence too? This question prompts the sub-title of this book.

In the fourth chapter I draw attention to a lesser known strand of modern thought represented by Hans Georg Gadamer among others (e.g., A. N. Whitehead and Lonergan). It denies that scientific knowing and managing represent all the ways we experience. It challenges the claims to hegemony of the technological, controlling orientation to reality identified and discussed above. It sees that orientation rather as partial and as an abstraction from the whole of what we do, undergo, and know as concrete selves, existing within the vital network of social relatedness. The technological orientation is a specialized affair; the broader picture is one characterized less by domination than dialogue. Moreover, the life of dialogue is seen to depend on and open out into ever wider horizons. It is within this context that talk of God finds its appropriate place.

The fifth and last chapter asks how God should be conceived. I identify and discuss a strand of contemporary Christian thought, inclusive of a variety of otherwise very different thinkers, which breaks with traditional theism in order to speak of God's perfection more in terms of God's capacity for reciprosity and social relatedness than in terms of sheer power and self-sufficiency. While there is no doubt much anthropomorphism in this way of thinking, as in all theology, it is a needed corrective. It suggests a way of relieving if not solving theodicical problems. Also, it suggests a way of seeing God and the world to be so intimately related, that the glorification of God and the love of the earth (and its inhabitants) need not be in competition: properly conceived, they are complementary.

As the broader understanding of human experience as dialogical includes but transcends the technological mode, the idea of God's perfection as social reciprocity includes but transcends the traditional emphasis on divine agency (control, immutability, etc.). In this way, one can come closer than before both to the Biblical vision of God as love and to the demands for justice voiced by thoughtful critics of religion in recent times. My argument, admittedly, has a programmatic character, but I believe it points out a promising and needed path of thinking that is responsive to current concerns of greatest import.

This book has as its ancestor the Samuel Ferguson Lectures at the University of Manchester which were my honor to deliver several years ago. I thank Dean A. O. Dyson and his colleagues in the faculty of theology and philosophy of religion, their students, and my hearers from the wider community for their cordial reception of my lectures and for the interesting discussions, formal and informal, which followed. I am especially grateful to Professor David A. Pailin for initially suggesting my name to the lectureship committee and who, with his wife Gwyneth, extended to me the gracious hospitality of their home throughout my days in Manchester. His thoughtful responses to my work and repeated urgings to publish it have also been appreciated.

I also recall with pleasure that my time in the United Kingdom included several days in Dublin, Ireland, where my host was The Reverend Professor Dermot Lane and where I was invited to address and discuss key ideas found in this book with students and faculty at the *Mater Dei* Institute and faculty and clergy from the area, especially from the universities of Dublin and Maynooth. My conversations in both Manchester and Dublin were as beneficial as they were enjoyable.

I also wish to express warm appreciation for the opportunity I had, in Montreal, to offer an interdisciplinary faculty seminar on Nietzsche, as well as to offer a course of lectures on Nietzsche to undergraduates during the academic year of 1991-92, the time of my tenure as Distinguished Visiting Scholar at Lonergan College, Concordia University. My second chapter in particular benefitted from that experience. I have fond memories of that year.

The argument of the book as a whole evolved out of

and was tested in the context of several seminars with my McMaster graduate students on the "Absence and Presence of God in Modern Culture." I will always remember with gratitude and affection those students and others whom it has been my privilege to teach (and from and with whom to learn) at McMaster.

McMaster University, my regular academic home for a quarter of a century, has provided rich opportunities for friendship and thought, in excess of my capacity to appropriate. A complete list of those to whom I am significantly indebted at McMaster and in Hamilton even in the last few years would be too great for recall here. It would include colleagues in my own and several other departments, including Professors Gerard Valée and Travis Kroeker, and also two clergy conversation partners, Rex Dolan and my wife and beloved companion, Joan. I also have appreciated ongoing conversations with my former classmate at Yale, Professor W. H. Austin, now a philosopher at the University of Houston, and my friends in good times and bad, Gilbert and Doris Ferrell and Mary and Charlie Pfeiffer. And not only for the sake of sentiment but also sober honesty, I must mention my sons, John Eric and Mark, for I recall how often shared meals became symposia and walks in the woods became dialogues in the truest sense.

The preparation of the manuscript is indebted to Jeannie Salamy, who skillfully and patiently translated my bad handwriting into typescript and to Daniel Leister and Susan Tweeny for stylistic suggestions and technical assistance. I also thank Dikran Y. Hadidian of Pickwick Publications for his patience and professional helpfulness.

Finally, I wish to thank in a very special way Professors Michael Welker of the University of Heidelberg in Germany and Ben Meyer of McMaster. I have benefitted from many hours of serious and joyful conversation over the years with each about philosophical and theological matters, including more recently those discussed in this book, and both have taken time from their own work to give me the very great benefit of their close and thoughtful reading of the entire manuscript. I am enormously grateful to them. They should be exonerated, of course, from my failure to learn even more from them than I have.[5] I have sometimes chosen to think and write what they would not.

These are many expressions of gratitude for a short book, but even so it is overly restrictive for practical reasons. For all those named and others simply thought of, it is no mere duty but a great joy to express heartfelt appreciation.

John C. Robertson, Jr.
Dundas, Ontario
November, 1994

NOTES

1. C. S. Lewis, *A Mind Awake: An Anthology of C. S. Lewis*, ed. Clyde S. Kilby (London: Geoffrey Bles, 1968), 219-252.

2. Pitirim Sorokin, *The Crisis of our Age* (New York: E.P. Dutton and Co., 1942), 303. David B. Barrett, *World Christian Encyclopedia: A Comparative Study in Churches and Religions A.D. 1900-2000* (New York: Oxford University Press, 1982).

4. Van A. Harvey, *The Historian and the Believer: The Morality of Historical Knowledge and Christian Belief* (Philadelphia: The Westminster Press, 1966), passim, esp. 102-126.

5. I regret that I had not yet had an opportunity to ponder, at the time of my writing, Michael Welker's recent *God the Spirit*, trans. by John F. Hoffmeyer (Minneapolis: Fortress Press, 1994) and Ben Meyer's *Reality and Illusion in New Testament Scholarship: A Primer in Critical Realist Hermeneutics* (Collegeville, MN: Liturgical Press, 1994).

I

SCIENTIFIC OBJECTIVISM

A friend tells of having the wonder, caused by the spectacle of the starry heavens above on a clear summer night, interrupted by a young son's question, "Dad, which ones of those did we put up there?" Similarly, if older people still theologize about the end of the world, the apocalypse envisioned by the young is of a different sort. It is difficult to say when exactly the modern Western world came into being. While it is known for many remarkable things, including the abolition of slavery and the birth of individualism, can there be any doubt that, its distinguishing features are its science and technology?

Other societies, to be sure, have had science. The ancient Greeks did. So did the great Asian civilizations. But in our era—with its reversal of the flow of great rivers, landings on the moon, splitting the atom, and manipulations of the genetic code—we can hardly doubt that science has affected our society in a way previously unequaled. Nor can we doubt that in our society, science has captured the popular imagination, and scientists have achieved previously unmatched prestige and authority. Moreover, there is the widespread conviction in our society that our science is different in both quality and kind from previous science, so that one can speak of a distinctively modern science.

What is it that sets our science apart from earlier science, as being not only better but also different? Since Descartes in the 17th century, we have grown accustomed to answering this question by pointing to method, to modern, scientific method. It has been argued that the astonishing progress modern science has made can be traced certainly not to the superior talents or efforts of modern scientists, but rather to the discovery of a particular method—a method which can be uniformly and collaboratively applied and which yields tangible, cumulative, and publicly verifiable results. This modern scientific method it has been thought—again since Descartes and more recently since Comte in the 19th century and the Vienna Circle in the 20th—might well be applied not only to physical nature but to everything, as a key to success and progress in the social sciences and social engineering analogous to that possible in mathematics and physics.

By focusing on this magic word "method," we can best understand the present state of the notorious "warfare" between science and religion. We can now see that this is the real point of conflict. We can distinguish between basic and less-than-basic conflicts. In the category of less-than-basic, we can include conflicts over the dating of particular events, such as the beginning of life, especially human life, and the universe itself. To be sure, controversies over Darwin and Dr. Hoyle do occur, so obviously they can, but these might be avoided, at least on the levels and in the areas where they characteristically occur, primarily because many religious people have learned to differentiate between piety, including respect for Biblical authority, and literalistic interpretations of scripture.

Nor need there be irresolvable conflicts over the physical character of those reported events which seem to violate scientific laws, i.e., miracles. For, on the one hand, religious people are now less adamant than in bygone days about equating the existential and literal meanings of events and, on the other hand, many philosophically sophisticated scientists (and historians) are much more cautious and tentative than before in their pronouncements about natural and historical laws. One should certainly not think, of course, that the bars are down to anything like a pre-critical belief in miracles, but the tension has eased enough to the degree and in such a way that a head-on conflict between scientific and religious mindedness is avoidable in this area.

Nor need there be basic collisions between religion and modern science over astronomy, for modern believers have learned to distinguish between the real intent of the scriptural message and the pre-scientific worldviews that provided its contexts. (Moreover, historically-minded ages have learned to regard all worldviews as provisional, revisable, and even fated for revision.)

There is nothing to be gained by oversimplifying the issues involved in conflicts of this kind. The point is simply to relativize them, to say that they are not areas of fundamental conflict. Now I do not wish to offer one more cheap and shallow attempt to make peace between science and religion (e.g.,"science deals with facts, religion with values," or "some call it evolution, and some call it God"). Religious people do make claims about intramundane events which may conflict with the judgments of natural scientists and critical historians. Furthermore, it may well be that science implies some metaphysical claims (and that some philosophically-minded scientists sometimes go beyond their particular science to try to say what they are), which may involve conflicts with some of the metaphysical claims of a religion. What I am saying, however, is that the *central* and *basic* area of conflict is not one in which certain scientific conclusions can be pitted against certain factual claims made by religion. Scientists are less dogmatic than before as to what might happen, and religious people are less dogmatic about what did happen.

Rather, the central and basic conflict is the one that would pit scientific method against religious claims about God. If modern science is tentative about its conclusions, it is not tentative about its method. Similarly, while a believer's commitment to any given factual claim may be soft, commitment to certain claims about God are not. Christians, Jews, and Muslims could not be what they are apart from their belief in God. The problem is, that scientifically-minded people doubt, first, that such claims can meet the demands of scientific method and, second, that such claims can be vindicated as meaningful in any other way. Here then is the area of fundamental conflict.

Nor is it the case that the difficulties in reconciling religion with the scientific method would concern only that special group of people who are actually scientists, for the prestige of science is such that what scientists are known to favor usually wins a place in the thinking of the general public, and what is dismissed by scientists loses its credibility.

Nor is it surprising that the culture at large should be captivated by whatever method lies at the core of science. Its achievements have been spectacular and have affected every aspect of our lives. The dream of isolating, grasping, and developing the new method has been irresistible. So has the dream of its universal application. Its universal application might allow us to unify the sciences. Homogeneous results might allow us to understand not only the laws of nature but those of the mind. We might furthermore have a clearing house for claims to truth, that would allow us to arrest and eliminate all unwarranted beliefs and assertions. We might find a way of achieving cumulative results in knowing what can be known. If only the golden key of method could be firmly grasped!

It is in this context that the example of Descartes (1596-1650)—commonly regarded as the begetter of modern philosophy—comes naturally and forcefully to mind. For it was the ideal of a *"science admirable,"* a new unified and all-encompassing science based on an exact mathematical-geometrical method, that came to him during the winter of 1619 and controlled the rest of his life. If only such an ideal could be articulated and followed in philosophy, the achievements of Copernicus, Kepler, Galileo and the modern geometers might be matched in other areas of thought (previously characterized, said Descartes, "more by words than by things").[1]

Again, there comes to mind Auguste Comte (1798-1857), founder of "positivism," who celebrated the discovery of scientific method as the third and highest stage of a three-part drama played out in history. Like Hegel (and modernity in general) he saw everywhere a progressive unfolding. The first historical stage he took to be that of theology and myth, followed by the stage of metaphysics, that in turn was supplanted by positive science. A new capacity to foresee, plan, and control ended the need for religion and ushered in a new age of humanity. Indeed Comte spoke energetically of himself despite persecution, as a prophet of a new *religion de l'humanité,* based on the new and solid foundations of positive science and technology.[2]

In our own century, there is little doubt that the most prominent seeker and representative of modern scientific methodologism has been not a single person, but a group—the so-called Vienna Circle. Founded in 1922 by Moritz Schlick, a pupil of the great physicist Max Planck, the Circle flourished through that intellectually remarkable decade, the 1920's. Composed almost exclusively of mathematicians, natural scientists, economists, logicians, and philosophers of science, the Circle published a manifesto, "Scientific Theory of the World—the Vienna Circle" (1929). In this and other documents the Circle expressed its intention to give an account of science that would do justice to the central importance of logic, mathematics, and theoretical physics. The group had little interest in the history of science, logic, or philosophy, emphasizing rather the radical break which their grasp of the scientific method allowed and required. The names of Hume, Mill, Helmholtz, Mach, and Poincaré were often invoked. The Circle especially admired and expounded the intellectual world of Frege, Russell, the "early" Whitehead, and the Wittgenstein of the *Tractatus Logico-Philosophicus* (1921)—a difficult and enigmatic work destined for extraordinary fame in the remaining years of the century. Perhaps Wittgenstein, who was not an actual member of the group, influenced the Circle more than anyone else. For despite Wittgenstein's mystical tendencies, which attracted the attention and worried some members of the Circle, most members found much in

Wittgenstein to admire, emulate, and advocate. There was a sense of an intrepid new beginning and insouciant indifference to tradition; attention was given to language, mathematics, and natural science, as opposed to metaphysics. There was a sense of having discovered a foundation, not so much in a doctrine as in a program, a method for saying what could be said and eliminating systematically what could not or ought not be said. They thought they saw in the *Tractatus* a rigorous empiricism, and something like what came to be known as the "verification principle," namely a distilled scientific method.

The general idea of the principle was not difficult to
        Whether Wittgenstein actually taught the verification principle is debatable; however, the principle soon came to be regarded as the Vienna Circle's leading insight. The discovery of the principle, it was thought, was the discovery of that feature of modern science that made it so successful. It would at last be possible to finish with the endless debates about meaning and truth at one stroke by supplying a criterion for meaningful assertions, thus separating sense from nonsense.[3]

        The general idea of the principle was not difficult to state, but precise formulation required continual revision. The aim was to rule out bogus truth-claims without also eliminating much natural science and common sense. Rudolf Carnap (1891-1970) and A. J. Ayer (1911-1991) were the leaders in the attempt to refine the principle, and the second edition (1946) of Ayer's *Language, Truth and Logic* was commonly regarded as the definitive formulation of the principle. In this book, Ayer says:"a statement is held to be literally meaningful if and only if it is either analytic or empirically verifiable."[4] If it is analytic (e.g., a definition or a mathematical statement), then it tells us nothing factual about the world. If it asserts something factual about the world, it must ultimately be based upon sense experience. If a statement which claims to tell us what is so about something is to be meaningful, one must be able to deduce from it observational consequences. This does not mean that I must be able to see an atom in order to make meaningful assertions about it; however, it is required that I be able to specify some entailed factual consequences that can be seen or heard, etc. Ideas must, in other words, be traceable to discreet *sensa*.

An important mutation in this general stream of thought occurred with Karl Popper[5]. Although sympathetic to the goals of Carnap and Ayer and the Circle in general, Popper found the celebrated Verification Principle overly restrictive. He found that it, in effect, eliminated all scientific and natural laws, inasmuch as their claims to universality could never be matched by empirical experiences, whose numbers must always be finite. In other words, a claim such as "electrons have a charge of so many C.G.S. electrostatic units" or, for that matter, "salt is soluble in water" can not be regarded as meaningful according to the Verification Principle, for it is obviously impossible to test *all* electrons or *all* salt.

Furthermore, Popper argued, the principle would be stultifying if followed, for even sense perceptions are interpreted in light of inherited assumptions, imaginative leaps, or creative musings. No one can trace every idea to a substantiating sense experience. Yet Popper does not conclude from this that the quest for a criterion for meaningfulness is illegitimate. As a criterion, however, one should replace the method of verification with the method of *falsification*. A statement is *meaningful* if one can specify what observable states-of-affairs it rules out; that is, if one can say which possible state-of-affairs it falsifies, and which state-of-affairs then would in turn falsify it. Such a statement can be regarded as provisionally or tentatively valid or *true*, so long as such potentially falsifying states-of-affairs are, in fact, not discovered. For example, "all swans are white" is meaningful because one can specify a potentially falsifying observation ("here is a black swan") and it is a provisionally valid "conjecture" so long as a colored swan is not observed.

Now with this background in mind, we can turn to the well-known "Theology and Falsification" debate, which occurred in the 1950's and has set the tone of much philosophy of religion in the English speaking world since that time. The central piece in the discussion was a paper by the British philosopher, Antony Flew, first contributed to an Oxford University student publication and subsequently often reprinted, most notably in the volume *New Essays in Philosophical Theology*.[6] Flew's contribution took the form of a challenge to theologians, a challenge of a Popperian sort. The challenge had to do with the meaningfulness of religious claims concerning the existence and attributes of God, especially claims about divine power and goodness, and it consisted largely of asking religious believers to specify "what would have to occur, or to have occurred, to constitute for you a disproof of the love of, or of the existence of, God?" In other words, Flew challenged those interested in making assertions about God to specify potentially falsifying observations or to surrender the pretense of speaking meaningfully. More particularly, Flew's challenge had a theodicical edge:

> Now it often seems to people who are not religious as if there was no conceivable event or series of events the occurrence of which would be admitted by sophisticated religious people to be a sufficient reason for conceding "There wasn't a God after all"or "God does not really love us then". Someone tells us that God loves us as a father loves his children. We are reassured. But then we see a child dying of inoperable cancer of the throat. His earthly father is driven frantic in his efforts of help, but his Heavenly Father reveals no obvious sign of concern. Some qualification is made—God's love is "not a merely human love'or it is 'an inscrutable love", perhaps—and we realize that such sufferings are quite compatible with the truth of the assertion that "God loves us as a father (but, of course,....)." We are reassured again. But then perhaps we ask: What is this assurance of God's (appropriately qualified) love worth, what is this apparent guarantee really a guarantee against? Just what would have to happen not

> merely (morally and wrongly) to tempt but also
> (logically and rightly) to entitle us to say "God
> does not love us" or even "God does not ex-
> ist"?[7]

Since the original piece appeared, Flew and his followers (e.g., Kai Nielsen) have developed and refined this
challenge in a variety of forms and contexts and with ingenious variations, but basically with the same bite: specify
what observable fact or state-of-affairs would count against
your assertions, or surrender the claim that they are cognitively meaningful.

The responses to Flew's challenge have been nu-
merous, often lively, and also ingenious (although almost
entirely limited to the English-speaking world). Surprising-
ly enough, however, most of these responses are variations
of one of the two early responses.

On the one hand, there has been a sort of "left-
wing" or non-cognitivist response, the most notable example of which has probably been R. B. Braithwaite's *An Empiricist's View of the Nature of Religious Belief*,[8] (but one
should also mention Paul van Buren of the United States
and Don Cupitt in England).[9] In this small book Braithwaite is willing to waive the claim that religious statements
qualify as meaningful factual assertions: they are not testa-
ble by observation, they are compatible with every conceivable state of affairs (hence are non-falsifiable), and, like the
necessary statements of logic and mathematics, they make
no assertion of existence. Though cognitively empty, however, religious assertions can nevertheless be shown to be
meaningful—in the sense of useful.

Religious statements, according to Braithwaite's account, can be seen as ways of expressing a user's commitment to a particular course of action or way of life. In this
way, religious statements resemble moral statements, differing for the most part only in the manner of expression: moral statements are more direct and refer to general principles, whereas religious language usually takes a narrative
form. Because religious and moral statements serve to express intentions and ground conduct, they cannot be dis-

missed as meaningless. In this, Braithwaite's position follows that of the "later" Wittgenstein who altered the verification principle in the direction of the "use-principle," according to which the meaning of any statement is found by attending to the way it is used in ordinary discourse. Accordingly, even though religious statements are nonsensical in the literal sense, they cannot be dismissed as nonsense in the pejorative sense. So Braithwaite, and the "left-wing" in general, rescued religious statements from the tough-minded positivist's trash basket—but only at the exorbitant price of admitting that such statements are cognitively empty.

On the other hand, there has been a "right wing" response to Flew, which has consisted of attempting to show that religious statements are cognitively meaningful because they are indeed factual. For example, Basil Mitchell agreed with the demands of the falsification principle, namely, that an assertion must imply some possible state-of affairs which would, if actual, count against its truth.[10] Mitchell allows, for example, that instances of evil count against the statement that God loves the world. Nevertheless, instances of evil do not simply and as such *decisively* count against (i.e., falsify) the statement, "God loves the world,"unless it can be shown that there are no plausible excuses for a specified instance of evil. Mitchell offered an analogy of a member of the Resistance who, on the basis of an encounter, comes to trust a stranger as a friend and ally. Such trust was reinforced by some of the stranger's subsequent deeds. And the trust was perhaps disturbed but not overturned by the stranger's occasionally ambiguous actions or inaction, because in each instance the member could believe that there must have been extenuating circumstances and plausible excuses.

Flew's rejoinder was incisive and potent.[11] On the one hand, he commended Mitchell for agreeing, first, that religion makes and implies assertions and, second, that if assertions are to be assertions, "there must be something that would count against their truth." On the other hand, he

rejected Mitchell's recourse to "possible saving explanations" in dealing with the theodicy issue by rejecting the
applicability of Mitchell's analogy. "We cannot," wrote
Flew, "say that (God) would like to help but he cannot: God
is omnipotent. We cannot say that he would help if he only
knew, for God is omniscient." Of course, observed Flew,
one can always avoid the disconfirmation of an hypothesis
by inventing qualifications and arbitrary sub-hypotheses,
but only at the price of allowing the central terms "to die
the death of a thousand qualifications" and the hypothesis
itself to degenerate into vacuity.

An interesting variation on Mitchell's sort of defence has been that of John Hick.[12] According to Hick, the
Christian faith is factually meaningful because it can be
verified in the afterlife, i.e., eschatologically. Hick did not
try to prove that God exists and has certain attributes; rather
he dealt with the logically prior issue of whether statements
about God are so much as meaningful. Hick did not, of
course, argue that God could be directly experienced by
one of our five senses. His argument, rather, was that Christian belief in God would be confirmed if after death we
could experience ourselves in a community composed of
members of our family, friends, and historical figures
known to be dead under the rule of Jesus Christ. This
would provide a "weak" or indirect kind of confirmation of
the central theological claim.

Perhaps the key rejoinder to Hick's kind of eschatological verification theory has been that of the Canadian
Kai Nielsen.[13] The gravamen of Nielsen's complaint is that
the theory has a conceptually confused quality about it. For
one thing, while we know what it is to identify other people
in this life, what would it mean to speak of observing and
identifying not ordinary bodies, but "resurrection bodies" in
a "celestial city"? For another thing, even if we could observe "resurrection bodies," how would this support claims
about a non-anthropomorphic and transcendent God who in
principle cannot be observed? In other words, Nielsen's position posits that it is meaningless to speak of "indirectly

verifying" something that cannot even in principle be directly verified.

The philosopher R. M. Hare remarked over 25 years ago that "on the ground marked out by Flew, he seems to me to be completely victorious."[14] What is strange, it seems to me, is that the great majority of those who have responded to Flew's challenge since it was first issued in the mid 1950's have agreed to confine themselves to just this ground. That has, however, been the case; for both the "left" and "right" wing have agreed that necessary truths are existentially empty and that all existential claims must be subject to falsification if not to decisive verification: that is, they must be contingent. The difference between the "left" and "right" is that the former have been willing to concede that religious assertions are cognitively meaningless, but have held that they are meaningful in some other way, and the latter have sought to show that religious assertions are meaningful because they are factual.

What is strange about this is that Flew's "marking out" of the ground was in effect only a retracing of the boundaries staked out by the Vienna Circle and its successors, whose dominant passion was to limit meaning and truth to the mathematical and scientific and to exclude, systematically, the metaphysical and theological.

Of course, Flew's lineage antedates the Vienna Circle. It goes back at least as far as David Hume who wrote in a celebrated passage:

> When we run over to our libraries, persuaded of these principles, what havoc must we make? If we take in our hand any volume; of divinity or school metaphysics, for instance; let us ask, Does it contain any abstract reasoning concerning quantity or number? No. Does it contain any experimental reasoning concerning matter of act and experience? No. Commit it then to the flames; for it can contain nothing but sophistry and illusion.[15]

In this passage, Hume supplied the Western world

with a two-pronged "fork" for spearing the cognitively meaningful. What was neither analytically true nor a matter of contingent fact observable by the senses was to be counted as refuse. As we have seen, there have been those who have tried—valiantly perhaps—to justify theological discourse in terms of these criteria. While it has not been obvious to all that the attempts have been outright failures, for many they have lacked persuasive force and have seemed unreal. Perhaps Gilbert Ryle's response to this situation is understandable (if lamentable):

> The theological fire has died down, but it has not quite gone out and the kettle of theological philosophy, though far from even simmering, is not quite stone cold. Some philosophers, some of the time, do take some interest in tensions between theological, scientific, and moral ideas. Others are at least polemically interested enough to deny that theological dictions convey any ideas at all. But most of us, most of the time, do just forget about the subject.[16]

If these efforts to justify theological truth-claims "on the ground marked out by Flew" have seemed to many people unreal and lacking in force, the reason may have more to do with the nature of the religious subject-matter than anything else. Put differently, it should have been clear from the beginning that Flew's ballfield was too small an area on which to play a theological language game. Or to change metaphors, we should have known from the outset that we could not eat theological fare with Hume's two-pronged fork—and not because the fare is too thin (or nonexistent), but because the instrument is inept. This, at any rate, is the common lesson taught by at least three important 20th century studies on the work of a medieval monk, St. Anselm, and his account of the "logic of God." I refer to the studies of Karl Barth, Charles Hartshorne, and Norman Malcolm.[17]

Despite the great differences between Barth, the Protestant theologian, Hartshorne, the process philosopher, and Malcolm, the linguistic analyst, they all came independently to approximately the following arresting and *common* conclusion: Anselm has shown us that we cannot speak about God as though God's existence were a contingent fact. A person may, of course, choose not to speak of God at all. Or a person may choose to say that "God exists" is *necessarily* false (e.g., because a contradictory or incoherent idea). *Or* one may say that the statement "God exists" is *necessarily* true. What one cannot say, however, is that God exists contingently. That is, while one can meaningfully say of a stone or star or any other finite being that it "still exists" or "may someday come to exist" or "no longer exists," one cannot, without exposing one's insensitivity to the meaning of the word, say any of these things of God. God either necessarily (and hence eternally) does not exist or necessarily (and hence eternally) does exist. What God can not do is happen to exist or not exist; in other words, it cannot merely be a contingent fact that God exists. God does not exist in the way a thing does.

Of course, for a long time, the conventional opinion has been that Anselm (a) failed to distinguish between merely logical or conceptual possibilities and real possibilities, and that he (b) mistakenly concluded from God's perfection to God's existing inasmuch as a non-existence would be an imperfection unworthy of God. To the former Aquinas and others have argued that real possibilities are neither the same as nor deducible from merely logical possibilities, and Gaunilion, Kant, and others have argued that existence is not a predicate. What Barth, Hartshorne, and Malcolm—for all their considerable differences—have discovered, however, is that the logic of our discourse about God cannot be the same as our discourse about things. Moreover, Anselm's point was not that mere existence is a predicate, but that *necessary* existence is a predicate of divine perfection. It is a uniqueness of the name "God" that it can be used properly only to refer to a necessarily existing Being or not at all. To speak of a God who just happens to exist is to speak in violation of the "depth grammar" of the word, God.

Therefore, not only can one not specify observations which would directly verify statements about a transcendent God, neither can one speak of states-of-affairs which would falsify a claim such as "God exists." For if God necessarily exists, then no state-of-affairs could prevent or rule out God's existence. To assume otherwise is to assume that God's existence is a contingent fact and not the ground of all facts and all possible facts ("of all things visible and invisible," as the Nicene Creed states).

When one is committed, therefore, to a principle or method according to which necessary truths can only be non-existential and existential truths can only be contingent, it is a foregone conclusion that talk of God will become increasingly unreal, since talk of necessary existence is ruled out from the start. What is the status, however, of just this rule or method? (As Wittgenstein came to see, something can only be so much as a mistake within a particular system.)

Precisely this question was the topic of a 1949 debate between Ayer and the historian of philosophy, Frederick Copleston.[18] Copleston challenged the view that positivism's verification/falsification principle was a "neutral" technique. The principle, Copleston argued, cannot itself be justified according to its own criteria, precisely because it is neither analytically true nor a verifiable empirical hypothesis. Rather it is, he concluded, a *proposal* as to what we should regard as real. Ayer seemed only to be able to answer the charge by insisting, in effect, that the proposal was a good and useful one.

Instructively, we find Carl Hempel coming to the same understanding. In an early statement (1951) he spoke of the imminent articulation of the verificationist principle which would pave the way for progress in rationality. In a later statement (1966) he admitted that it was becoming clear that there were difficulties in stating the principle in a way that avoided the charge of vicious circularity and question-begging. Then still later he dolefully and humbly concludes that the principle really has the logical status of a proposal as to what we *should* hereafter regard as rational.[19]

One may want to ask further, however, about the proposal and its presuppositions, for as the New England poet, Robert Frost, has said about fences, when building a fence, one should ask not only what is being fenced in but also what is being fenced out. Obviously what the verificational/falsification principle wished to fence in, was the scientific method, thereby capturing and harnessing its astonishing power to grasp and control objects. What was fenced out, not by accident, but by design, was speech about God.

But that is not all that was fenced out. Although scientific positivism began with implied criticisms of what the positivists correctly identified as dangerous ideological tendencies in the pre-World War II European climate, it was a notorious fact that their method made no provision for moral truth claims, whether they be those advanced by the executioners or the victims, the collaborators or the resisters.

Nor were God and morality the only things that became unreal with positivism. As their grip on "objects" became tighter and tighter, the subjects that they and we are, have seemed to become increasingly vague. The self has begun to disappear. It was symbolic that Russell corrected Descartes' "I think" to read "It thinks within me." He was followed in turn by Carnap, who—maintaining that "the existence of the self is not an originally given fact"—struck out the 'within me'."[20]

In one sense this conclusion is not strange, for once one limits the real to the observable *sensa*, then one will never find the self. Perhaps we will recall the comic parable of the man who raced outside to peer in the window to see if he was at home. In another sense, however, the conclusion is very strange. The modern scientific age was generated by the genius and mighty mental labor of deeply theological men such as Kepler and Copernicus. Yet the result has been a scientistic ideology which has a place neither for God nor the human self. It is a mighty movement that remarkably exhibits the power of the mind and yet leads to the denial of the mind itself, thus creating the spectacle of an offspring that has no place for the parent.

Aristotle observed in his *Nicomachean Ethics* that "it is the mark of an educated mind to expect that amount of exactness in each kind which the nature of the particular subject admits." (Bk. I, 1094, b25). When we make extraordinary demands for exactness on reality, something may indeed be revealed but much also may be concealed.

As the 20th century winds down, it is clear that the crucial issue of our time was not the struggle between capitalism and communism; it was and is the common and great struggle to come to grips with the meaning of modern science and technology.

On the one hand, there is no denying that it is science and technology that make possible mass production, without which the world could not begin to be fed and clothed. On the other hand, modern science and technology have seemed to have unleashed the ravenous appetites of mass consumption, the demands of which apparently exceed even our enormous capacities to produce with the resulting epidemic of world hunger and environmental devastation.

Again, while there has been deliverance from superstition, our prejudices are armed as never before, we have become rootless, and thus vulnerable to the tyranny of powerful media manipulation, and to the nihilistic power of impersonal processes which seem beyond our control. This does not mention the threat of nuclear blackmail, or actual nuclear annihilation.

The successes cause us to respect our science and its method, but as we approach the end of one century and contemplate the prospects for the next, we ask: "Is this scientific method all it is touted to be?" "Is it capable of telling us all the truth and all the sorts of truths we need to know?" Is it providing all the inspiration, strength, and nourishment we require, if we are to live wisely and well, indeed if we are even to survive?

NOTES

1. This story is told well by Hans Küng in his *Does God Exist? An Answer for Today*, trans. Edward Quinn (Garden City, New York: Doubleday and Co., 1980), 3-41.

2. August Comte, *The System of Positive Philosophy* (New York: Burt Franklin, 1968).

3. For a good, brief account of the history of logical positivism and the Vienna Circle, see Alfred J. Ayer, "Introduction" in *Logical Positivism*, ed. with intro. A. J. Ayer (New York: The Free Press, 1959), 3-28. See also R.W. Ashby, "Verifiability Principle" in: *Encyclopedia of Philosophy*, ed. Paul Edwards, et al. (New York: Macmillan Publishing Co. and the Free Press; London: Collier Macmillan Publishers, 1967), vol. 8, 240-247.

More recently, "logical positivism" has come to be included as a species under the genus of "evidentialism" and "foundationalism." According to the latter terms, a belief is thought to be rationally justified if and only if it is itself built on a self-verifying sensory experience or is logically implied or entailed by such a belief. See D. Z. Phillips, *Faith After Foundationalism* (London; New York: Routledge, 1988), 3 and *passim*. See also *Faith and Rationality*, eds. Alvin Plantinga and Nicholas Wolterstorff (Notre Dame; London: University of Notre Dame Press, 1983), 1-16.

4. Alfred J. Ayer, *Language, Truth and Logic* (New York: Dover Publications, 1946),

5. Karl Popper, *The Logic of Scientific Discovery* (London: Hutchinson and Co., 1959).

6. *New Essays in Philosophical Theology*, eds. Antony Flew and Alasdair McIntyre (London: SCM Press, 1955).

7. Flew and McIntyre, *New Essays*, 98. In Chapter V, we will see that there are those theologians who argue that Flew's type of criticism is attacking a naive idea of omnipotence.

8. R. B. Braithwaite, *An Empiricist's View of the Nature of Religious Belief* (Cambridge: Cambridge University Press, 1955).

9. Paul M. van Buren, *The Secular Meaning of the Gospel* (New York: Macmillan; London: Collier-Macmillan, 1963). Donald Cupitt, *On Taking Leave of God* (London: SCM Press, Ltd., 1980).

10. Flew and MacIntyre, *New Essays*, 102-104.

11. Flew and MacIntyre, *New Essays*, 104-107.

12. John Hick, "Theology and Verification," *Theology Today*, 17 (1960), 12-31.

13. Kai Nielsen, "Eschatological Verification," *Canadian Journal of Theology*, 9 (1963), 271-281.

14. Flew and MacIntyre, *New Essays*, 99.

15. David Hume, *Enquiries concerning Human Understanding and Concerning the Principles of Morals*, ed. L.A. Selby-Bigge (Oxford: Clarendon Press, 2nd ed., 1902), 165. I do not mean, of course, to imply that the Vienna Circle added nothing to Hume. Hume looks simple and a bit rough-hewn when compared to the Circle. However, the Circle's work is anticipated by Hume.

16. Gilbert Ryle, "Final Discussion" in *The Nature of Metaphysics*, ed. D. F. Pears (London: Macmillan, 1957), 160. Quoted by Malcolm L. Diamond in *The Logic of God: Theology and Verification*, ed. by Malcolm L. Diamond and Thomas V. Litzenburg, Jr. (Indianapolis: The Bobbs-Merrill Company, Inc., 1975), 51.

17. Karl Barth, *Fides quaerens intellectum: Anselm's Beweis der Existenz Gottes* (Zürich: Evangelischer Verlag,1913, ET, Pickwick Publications, 1985). Charles Hartshorne, *Anselm's Discovery: A Re-Examination of the Ontological Proof of God's Existence* (LaSalle, Ill.: Open Court, 1965). Norman Malcolm "Anselm's Arguments," *Philosophical Review*, 69 (1960), 42-52.

18. "Logical Positivism—a Debate," Third Program, British Broadcasting Corporation (June 13, 1949), by Alfred J. Ayer and Frederick C. Copleston, S.J. Reprinted in Diamond and Litzenburg, eds., *L.G.*, 98-118.

19. Malcolm L. Diamond, "Introduction" in *L.G.*, 36f.

20. William Barrett, *Death of the Soul: From Descartes to the Computer* (Garden City, New York: Doubleday, Anchor Press, 1986), passim.

II

HUMANISTIC SUBJECTIVISM

In reply to the question as to what he might say if, at the divine judgment seat after his death, he found himself having to answer for his disbelief, Lord Russell is supposed to have said that he would say, "God, you just did not give us enough evidence." A contrasting story concerns Voltaire who is reported to have said, with eyes ablaze, "Humanity will not be free until the last king is strangled with the entrails of the last priest."[1] The two apocryphal stories may serve to suggest the difference is tone and at least surface appearance of two prominent intellectual trends. The first, largely centered in the Anglo-Saxon world and discussed in the first chapter, is scientific in mood. Out of concern to get the facts straight concerning the external world, it is sceptical about the God-hypothesis and indeed finally also about the self. The second trend, largely centered in continental Europe and now also prominent in the Third World will be the topic of this chapter. It begins with a passionate concern for the selfhood of the self, and with equal passion denounces belief in God as one of the impediments to human liberation, indeed as the chief impediment.

To understand this stream of thought which had entered into the water of modernity in such a powerful way, we might well focus on Feuerbach, Marx, Freud, Hartmann, Dewey, Sartre, Camus, Bloch, or a number of others. I propose, however, with some hesitation, to center on Friedrich Nietzsche. I hesitate because of the many bad associations that will all but inevitably distort any hearing we might give Nietzsche. Nazis and other Fascists aided by the

perverse editing of his works, have so appropriated Nietzsche as to make it very difficult for the rest of us to understand the phrase "will-to-power" without thinking of tanks
and storm troopers. We have, moreover, no way to translate
"*Übermensch*" without calling to mind at best a comic strip
character named "Superman," or at worst wartime propa-
ganda used to justify extermination camps. The early trans-
lations of Nietzsche into English, furthermore, rendered his
virtually peerless German into a style of English that had
long since become passé and quaint to our ears.[2]

Nietzsche, however, despite such difficulties, is virtually unavoidable for us, for he has managed to gather up
and express so many of the themes characteristic of our era:
our historical-mindedness, our sense of cultural relativity,
our belief that the horizons of our culture are our own crea-
tions, and our suspicion that our basic convictions and
ideals are ideological projections onto an indifferent cosmos. Moreover, he has not only expressed but also stamped
our culture, if in no other way than by his influence on our
social scientists, through such disciples as Max Weber and
Max Scheler, who doubtless have had their influence on social policy, as well as on the general climate of opinion in
our universities and in society at large.[3] Above all, however, we focus on Nietzsche here, because he represents an
important kind of critique of religion, a critique that grows
out of an awesome labor on behalf of the human self, its
liberation and authenticity. Many well-known thinkers
could be mentioned in connection with this way of thinking, but none has struggled harder for the selfhood of individuals (at least for those he felt were capable of liberation), than the one who was called by his high school
classmates, the "little pastor."[4]

It is ironic, to be sure, to depict as a preacher one
who was to write pieces entitled, "The Anti-Christ" and
"Twilight of the Gods," and who aligned himself with "Di-
onysius against the Crucified." Nietzsche's life nonetheless
had a sort of prophetic form and passion. He toiled valiantly to fulfill something akin to a mission, that of liberating

"the elect" from the hold of a false consciousness which
was depriving them of their true potential full humanity.
Shortly before the mental collapse which claimed the last
decade of his relatively short life, Nietzsche wrote an auto-
biographical sketch of sorts entitled, Ecce Homo: How One
Becomes what One Is.[5] The title captures something of
Nietzsche's mission, namely that of assisting human beings
to come into their own: to take possession of their lives, so
as to become all that they can be. It was for the sake of this
affirmation of life that Nietzsche became such an astute,
fierce, and determined social critic and so resolute a foe of
classical philosophy and religion in general, and of Platon-
ism and Christianity in particular. The elite, Nietzsche believed, were trapped under a social canopy of meanings,
values, and alleged truths that were crippling their potential
and smothering their lives. It was to liberate these prisoners
that Nietzsche struggled in his writings. The prophetic analogy mentioned above can be pressed further, for Nietzsche's sense of mission was based upon something like a
revelation. He spoke of it as "the great noon," referring to
his insight into the true origin and function of values and
meanings.[6] He came to see, he believed, that the social canopy is hardly a part of the fabric of the heavens, as its apol-
ogists would have one believe. Rather, our social meanings
and values have "human, all-too-human" origins. This was
the conviction that gave direction and urgency to Nietzsche's work.

Since Nietzsche, the idea of projection has come to
be associated with Freud, and largely thanks to Freud's
popularity, the word has become a part of our everyday vo-
cabulary. Prior to Nietzsche, the word (Entäusserung) was
uncommon. We do find it gaining prominence in Marx,
who apparently learned it from Ludwig Feuerbach. Feuerbach, for his part, had developed the notion of projection,
in reacting against Hegel's tendency to swallow up the finite and human into the Infinite and Divine.[7] Feuerbach, as
Marx later said, stood the speculative and mystical Hegel
back on his feet. Hegel, Feuerbach argued, had it wrong-

end-up, topsy turvy. Finite consciousness is not to be sub-
sumed into the Infinite; the Infinite rather is to be dissolved
into the finite, the Absolute Spirit into the human consciousness. God is not the secret mystery of the human being; rather the human being is the explanation of God.

Feuerbach's account of religion was no less critical
than that of others of the time, but it was considerably sub-
tler than most.[8] While others might dismiss religion as delu-
sion, he saw it as a necessary stage in humanity's self-
discovery. We discover our own nature by first projecting it
outside of ourselves. This is what God is: the infinity of human consciousness, hypostatized, personified, projected.
God as person, for example, is the projection of our personal being.[9] God as mind is the projection of our intellectual
nature.[10] God as morally perfect is the projection of our own
conscience.[11] God as love is a projection of our own capacity to love.[12] God as triune is a projection of our social nature.[13] Contrary to the Bible, it is not God who created us,
but we who created God. Contrary to Hegel, it was not the
Absolute who projected us, but we who have projected the
Absolute.

For Feuerbach, however, this projecting is not nuga-
tory; rather it is a useful stage in the process of self-
discovery, for it is in seeing our own powers projected that
we come to know them. It is also, however, a stage which
must be surpassed. We must come to recognize the projections for what they are, otherwise we remain in false consciousness, and thereby in inauthenticity and alienation. As
long as we fail to recognize our projections as projections,
we are impoverished and remain estranged from our own
natures. When, however, we discover the inner secret of the
projections and come to recognize in them our own creative, inventive, and positive power, we can appropriate our
own natures and become reconciled with ourselves. Then,
says Feuerbach, we can turn from being "theologians into
anthropologists, from theophiles into philanthropists, from
[being] candidates for the hereafter into students of the here
and now, from [being] religious and political lackeys of the

heavenly and earthly monarchy and aristocracy into free, self-confident citizens of the world."[14]

Nietzsche, then, did not invent the projection theory. But if he did not invent it, he enriched it with a new motive. That motive was the will-to-power.[15]

What exactly is the will-to-power? Nietzsche asserts that it is the inner reality of all things—an assertion that, Heidegger claims, is Nietzsche's equivalent of a metaphysical principle. Be that as it may, however, the important point here is that Nietzsche accepts the notion that our ideas and values are our own projections and adds to this his proposal that the motivation for these projections is our will-to-power.[16]

Consider the case of values. By saying that values are projections, Nietzsche is breaking with the world of classical philosophy and religion, which thought in terms of an objective order, one, first of all, that exists independently of us and is of itself worthy of contemplation and, secondly, a reality that gives limits, shape, and direction to our lives. To add that the projecting is expressive of the will-to-power takes us even further from classical theory. It leads us to construe values as instrumental, in the service of power, preserving and enhancing it. Hence, values—nothing in themselves—are useful to us in our battle to master ourselves and our environment. They are means that we posit in order to become stronger. This view of values, their source and function, was, to repeat, destructive of classical consciousness. It was also productive of a new possibility: the free creation of values more in accord with the principle of the will-to-power.

Here is where Nietzsche's denunciation of Christianity becomes comprehensible. He accuses Christianity of camouflaging the real origin and function of values, with the fiction that they are part of the created order itself, supposedly rooted in the eternal law. Pious hoodwinking hid the fact that the origin of values is to be found in mediocrity. This leads to a second aspect of Nietzsche's critique. The higher type of human being generates values out of an abundance of strength and vitality; the mediocre do not. The latter create values out of ressentiment, rancour against the strong, the talented, and the privileged. Thus, the mediocre attempt to undercut and control the elite. They attempt to undercut them by denegrating their values. They attempt to control them by promoting their own "herd values" as binding upon all. This, admittedly, is not the herd's conscious strategy, but it is in fact what they do, covertly and indirectly. Their's is a sick and perverted expression of the will-to-power. Nietzsche's complaint is not that the herd or mediocre masses have their own values, but that they promote these values as though they had universal application, as though they applied to the elite as well as to themselves.[17]

Nietzsche, however, exhorts the elite to create values in keeping with their own robust vitality. They should not allow Christianity—"a defamation and pollution of life"—to seduce them.[18] Nietzsche longed for the values that strong instincts would create; he damned a Christianity suspicious of beauty, joy, spontaneity, and humour. He charged Christianity with crimes against the human spirit: it exacerbated feelings of guilt, encouraged mistrust of passion, preferred weakness to strength, surrender to assertiveness. It taught that life was a punishment, that happiness was suspect, that self-confidence was reprehensible and pride sinful. He accused Christianity of promoting peace at the expense of ecstacy, adventure, daring and achievement.[19] On behalf of sensuous joy and emotional depth, Nietzsche fought against a religion that tried to extirpate, rather than cultivate the passions, seemingly on the assumption that "only the castrated man is a good [one]."[20] Considering how much they speak of redemption, Christ's followers, he said, should look more redeemed. It is not, however, just Christian morals which the free person must transcend, but also, and above all, belief in God and "the other world," for this belief is the supreme expression of *ressentiment*. It grows out of anxiety in the face of real life. Belief in another, truer, and better world is a betrayal of the earth. Belief in God as invisible and unchanging is a slander against space and time, which are the conditions of life as we know it.[21] With God war is declared on life, nature, and the will to live! Belief in God distracts us from the here and now, thereby devaluing concrete existence in favor of an abstraction. Embracing God alienates us from both our bodies and the earth itself, thereby robbing us of opportunities for the growth and joy that come through the exercise and augmentation of our powers.

Nietzsche's writings are filled with so many criticisms of Christianity that we could hardly even begin to consider each individually. Their distinguishing character, however, can be summarized in such words as these from his own notebooks:

> The question of the mere "truth" of Christianity—whether in regard to the existence of its God or the historicity of the legend of its origin, not to speak of Christian astronomy and natural science—is a matter of secondary importance as long as the question of the value of Christian morality is not considered.[22]

Nietzsche continues,

> The whole absurd residue of Christian fable, conceptual cobweb spinning and theology does not concern us; it could be a thousand times more absurd and we would not lift a finger against it. But we do combat the ideal that, with its morbid beauty and feminine seductiveness, with its furtive slanderous eloquence appeals to all the cowardices and varieties of weary souls....[23]

What he hates most in Christianity, he tells us, is that it "wants to break the strong, that it wants to discourage their courage . . . poison and sicken the noble instincts."[24]

We can see, then, that Nietzsche's critique of Christianity consisted not so much of cool scepticism about its

truth-claims, as of passionate protest against what he took
to be its life-denying attitudes. One could say it was a moral critique, but only so long as one is clear that Nietzsche
was much less interested in opposing some values with others than in liberating and empowering the elite to create
their own values freely, that is, in accord with their will-to-
power.

There is one question that Nietzsche knew he had to
face. If the prevalent values are those of mediocrity and
weakness, why have they prevailed? He answered: because
they have been the values of the vast majority. Contrary to
Darwin, it is not the fittest who survive, but the most nu-
merous, for there is strength in numbers. But the potentially
good news of modernity is that the traditional values are
beginning to lose their hold on the majority. "The greatest
recent event—that 'God is dead,' that the belief in the
Christian God has become unbelievable—is already beginning to cast its first shadows over Europe," Nietzsche ex-
ults in *The Gay Science*.[25]

Doubtless the prophet-like character of the parable
of the "Madman" in *The Gay Science* is Nietzsche's self-
portrait.[26] He sees and understands something that is as in-
evitable as thunder after lightning: the unchaining of history from its classical moorings. The process is already un-
derway, for the "highest values are devaluing themselves."
This means that the valuing of truth, inculcated by Christianity, has led at last to an insight into the true nature of all
values, namely that they are relative and time-bound things,
created by humans and, therefore, quite properly for humans. While he believed himself to be one of the first to
have had this insight with clarity, Nietzsche believed that a
vast and growing number of people were beginning to
sense its truth implicitly in their muscles and bones, if not
yet explicitly in their minds.

Doubtless this insight had had its earlier phases. *Die
anthropologische Wende*, the turn from God and the cosmos to the self, had many causes and anticipations. For example, there was the practical exigence, caused by the war-

ring factions of Christendom, for nations to find a secular, this-worldly basis for government. This, was anticipated by Machiavelli's break with classical political philosophy, his relocation of the real on earth not in heaven, his development of guidelines for mastering chance and managing society "realistically." There was Descartes' turn to the ego cogito as the source of certainty, the chief sample of reality, and the privileged access to what is, and Kant who made this ego cogito the silent but constant presupposition of all truth-claims, who effected the celebrated "Copernican revolution" in consciousness and proclaimed the primacy of practical reason. Then there were Feuerbach, and his follower Marx, who proclaimed in words now familiar to us, "The philosophers have only interpreted the world in various ways. The point, however, is to change it." Finally, we should mention Schopenhauer, for whom will was fundamental and all else epiphenomenal. We mention these thinkers together since, for all their differences, they collectively constitute a mutation in the Western tradition, a shift of focus away from nature and God. The new starting point for thinking and acting is the human self, a self called on to play an ever more active role in its encounter with the world. There is, in all these thinkers, an evergrowing sense of the managerial and mastering power of the human agent. Nor is it unreasonable to assume that the shift we see in them from a classical to a modern, from a cosmocentric and theocentric to an anthropocentric way of thinking and feeling, is also to be found in the culture at large, even if in a less conscious and articulate form.

The expression "death-of-God" was Nietzsche's way of describing the result of this ongoing mutation within Western consciousness. It was a dramatic way of saying that the idea of God, along with other assumptions of classical consciousness, was becoming increasingly unreal to a modern humanity rising up into a sense of its own dominion. The suprasensory world (that is, God and values hitherto accepted as given) has progressively lost its obligatory character as human beings progressively realize their own creative power. Ideas and values which we recognize as created by ourselves can only have less authority than do we ourselves, for we freely generated them.

The prophet sees the far-off lightning before the masses hear the thunder. They may believe that they still believe in God; but the prophet senses the incongruity between a belief in God coming off the top of the head and a practical atheism arising deep within the heart and increasingly inscribed in everyday practice. He also sees that even those who deny God with both head and heart, may not yet understand the radical and far reaching consequences of their denial.

It is time to let Nietzsche himself speak through his well-known parable from *The Joyful Wisdom*:

> The Madman. Have you not heard of that madman who lit a lantern in the bright morning hours, ran to the market place, and cried incessantly, "I seek God! I seek God!" As many of those who do not believe in God were standing around just then, he provoked much laughter. Why, did he get lost? said one. Did he lose his way like a child? said another. Or is he hiding? Is he afraid of us? Has he gone on a voyage? or emigrated? Thus they yelled and laughed. The madman jumped into their midst and pierced them with his glances.
> "Whither is God" he cried. "I shall tell you. We have killed him—you and I. All of us are his murderers. But how have we done this? How were we able to drink up the sea? Who gave us the sponge to wipe away the entire horizon? What did we do when we unchained this earth from its sun? Whither is it moving now? Whither are we moving now? Away from all suns? Are we not plunging continually? Backward, sideward, forward, in all directions? Is there any up or down left? Are we not straying as through an infinite nothing? Do we not feel the breath of empty space? Has it not become colder? Is not night and more night coming on all the while? Must not lanterns be lit in the morning? Do we not hear anything yet of the noise of the grave-

diggers who are burying God? Do we not smell
anything yet of God's decomposition? Gods too
decompose. God is dead, God remains dead.
And we have killed him. How shall we, the
murderers of all murderers, comfort ourselves?
What was holiest and most powerful of all that
the world has yet owned has bled to death under
our knives. Who will wipe this blood off us?
What water is there for us to clean ourselves?
What festivals of atonement, what sacred games
shall we have to invent? Is not the greatness of
this deed too great for us? Must not we ourselves become gods simply to seem worthy of
it? There has never been a greater deed; and
whoever will be born after us—for the sake of
this deed he will be part of a higher history than
all history hitherto."
Here the madman fell silent and looked again at
his listeners; and they too were silent and stared
at him in astonishment. At last he threw his lan-
tern on the ground, and it broke and went out. "I
come too early," he said then; "my time has not
come yet. This tremendous event is still on its
way, still wandering—it has not yet reached the
ears of man. Lightning and thunder require
time, the light of the stars requires time, deeds
require time even after they are done, before
they can be seen and heard. This deed is still
more distant from them than the most distant
stars—and yet they have done it themselves."
It has been related further that on the same day
the madman entered diverse churches and there
sang his *requiem aetemam deo*. Led out and
called to account, he is said to have replied each
time, "What after all are these churches now if
they are not the tombs and sepulchers of
God?"[27]

For Nietzsche, the death of God was the good news
that accompanied the advent of modernity. It was not, however good news in any straight-forward, undialectical
sense. Feuerbach's simple relief at the disappearance of the
divine struck Nietzsche as naive and premature. Nietzsche
would have eagerly shared in Sartre's ridicule of those who
wished to be atheists "at the least possible expense,"[28] for it

was part of the greatness of Nietzsche to recognize the mo-
mentous and awesome character of the loss of God. Recall
especially the last of the three images he used to suggest
the consequences of this mutation in the Western tradition:
"What did we do when we unchained this earth from its
sun? . . . Whither are we moving now? Are we not plunging
continually? . . . Are we not straying as through an infinite
nothing?"

  If, for Nietzsche, the death of God did not necessarily imply progress, it certainly did mean change. Who
would direct the change, he asked. Who would seize the
moment and choose between possible futures? Would it be
those whom he contemptuously called "last men," who,
with religious surrogates tried to still the anxiety of a life
without God? In place of the kingdom of heaven, they believe in historical progress; in place of eternal blessedness
and joy, they believe in happiness for the greatest number;
for divine creativity they substitute business and fun; in
place of salvation they trust in economic law, Wagnerian
music, and nature romanticism. Or would the future belong
to the nihilists, their hearts chilled by the encounter with
the abyss, no longer able to believe in God or an eternal order? The nihilists would either fall into the despair of the
weak, or else blindly exercise will without purpose, for the
sake of willing, preferring to will nothing to not willing at
all.[29]

  Nietzsche conceded that it may well be to the last
men or to the nihilists that the future belongs, but, he asserted, neither could achieve true greatness. Greatness was re-
served for the Supermen *(Übermenschen)*. They alone can
face the abyss with "unblinking eye" and the "courage of
an eagle." They alone can create values freely, consciously
in accord with the will-to-power, out of the joy and vitality
of their own strength. These will be the representatives of
an authentic, new humanity. Others have created values un-
knowingly and with vitiated wills, under the spell of false
consciousness and in the bad faith of self-forgetfulness. But
the spell is broken and the door is open for an escape from

such inauthenticity into an age in which old values can be transvalued and new values can be forged, values in keeping with the potential human greatness of a privileged elite.

This Nietzschean strand of atheism differed greatly in tone and emphasis from the epistemologically-oriented strand discussed in the first chapter. Yet the difference is not absolute, for Nietzsche discusses issues of truth and knowledge in some detail.[30] He includes his account of truth and knowledge in his larger account of values and morality. Just as he breaks with the assumption that values are given and objectively grounded, so also he rejects the notion that truth is there, readymade and available. And just as he rejects the idea of morality as a matter of adjusting to a *given* order, so he rejects the idea of knowledge as a mirroring of pre-constituted reality. In both cases, human creativity is dominant. Truth is a value, which is not at all the same thing as saying that truth is being valued. Rather it is to say that truth is something that the will-to-power posits as useful for its own preservation and enhancement. With the disappearance of God goes the disappearance of an objective order which is knowable and good to know, leaving in its place a flux, a chaos, too varigated and unstable to be grasped in knowledge. All we can do is interpret it in ways that serve our will-to-power. Truth is a name for a useful or successful way of managing this booming, buzzing confusion or this indescribable, meaningless abyss. Knowledge is not a faithful replication of being, but a productive mastering of becoming. For Nietzsche this is what truth and knowledge had always been. But hitherto false consciousness had hidden from us its true nature and function. Now, with the "great noon," we have come to see the truth about truth: its fabricated character. The *Ubermensch* joyfully and consistently acknowledges *and* wills this conception of truth.

Nietzsche does, of course, run into paradoxes at this point. For it is hard to know what "consistently" might mean in so chaotic a universe—or what "universe" might mean for that matter. He recognizes this sort of difficulty, complaining somewhere that we have not yet learned to be atheists for we still seem to believe in grammar. Behind all names and logic, he insists, lies the activity of valuing, a process of mastering and conquering in the service of power. If Aristotle held that human beings are motivated by a disinterested desire to know, Nietzsche holds that the desire to know was itself motivated by a passion more primitive. Beyond the question of the correctness of knowledge is "[t]he question [as] to what extent [an idea] is life-advancing, life-preserving, species-preserving, perhaps even species-breeding."[31]

One is never done with Nietzsche. Before bringing this chapter to a close, however, I should like to repeat that it was to Nietzsche's merit that he expressed so well so many of the assumptions and convictions of our society. Though he ridiculed and condemned aspects of our civilization, he intended to lead his readers deeper into its basic movement and defining spirit.[32] He wished to clarify and to help appropriate such typically modern motifs as the primacy of willing, the drive to master human and non-human nature by scientific techniques, the primacy of becoming over being and possibility over actuality, the historicity of existence and relativity of perspectives, and the opposition between self-realization and belief in God. If one wants to understand our age, one cannot afford to bypass Nietzsche.

We must conclude with questions about this conception of things. Is it the living of a truly human life? Is the will-to-power adequate to the world that encounters us in everyday life? Does the will-to-power do justice to the integrity of the other, i.e., to the object in a "subject-object relationship?" Classical thinkers may well have been too inclined to focus on the objective world of nature or culture *simply as given*, and too little appreciative of the active role of the subject. Modern thinkers—Kant, Kierkegaard, Newman, Blondel, James, and Habermas—may well have been justified in correcting them. *Nevertheless, one cannot help wondering if Nietzsche has not made an overcorrection.* Something of the otherness of the other, whether a tree or a person, has been compromised by the proposed Nietzschean instrumentalism. If the positivists run the risk of losing the subject, Nietzsche runs the risk of losing the external world, dissolving it all into grist for our mill.

If this gives us a dubious understanding of the other, does it not also give us an incomplete account of our responsibilities? Nietzsche is at least partially convincing, because he articulates so well our rebellion against heteronomous inhibitions of liberty. He also gives voice to the intellectual overthrow of universal norms, fixed essences, and unchangeable patterns. In this, he allies himself with individualism in ethics, relativism in sociology, evolution in biology, the elimination of final and formal causes in the natural sciences. He also expresses our sense of power as, armed with technology, we confront nature and each other.

Does the notion of the human being as *homo faber* (or *homo technicus*) render the essence of the human? It renders an aspect of the human essence, one neglected, even suppressed, in pre-Enlightenment societies, as indeed it is suppressed in parts of the world today. The question, however, is whether the willing, making, and mastering aspects *essentially* define us. Are we individually capable of exercising sovereignty over all beings? Can authentic community life be rendered by an aggregate of power-seeking individuals? Is this not exclusive emphasis on willing merely, as we are coming to recognize more frequently, a male stereotype, adequate to the authentic humanity of no human, female or male?

Finally, this situation will not allow us to sleep well. Cries of exultation over new-found power are increasingly matched by groans of loss and anxiety. Our growing capacity to shape things as we will, has left us unsure as to how we *should* shape things. Genetic engineering gives us the power to make even human nature itself as we will. It tells us nothing of what true humanity requires. It gives us no wisdom with respect to what end human life is most fit. Freedom and power all but topple into the absurd. "Go, wonderous creature," mocked Alexander Pope: "teach

Providence to rule; then drop into thyself and be a fool."[33]
Neither can play providence nor need to. On the Nietzschean sort of account, says Austin Farrer,

> the sceptre of Providence is forced into our fin-
> gers; if we do not play providence to ourselves,
> no one will; there is no other God. The ordeal of
> Phaethon is ours; the reins are in our hands, the
> doors of dawn are open, and we must guide the
> chariot of the Sun. We must but it's absurd; our
> ignorance, our liability to passion, the mutual
> frustration of our aims, present the spectacle of
> forty Phaethons drunk, driving wild on the
> Place de Concord.[34]

Finally, there is a question not only to Nietzschean
humanism, but to all the representatives of atheistic humanism: How can the phrase "atheistic humanism" fail to be
self-contradictory? In the dialogue between humanism and
theistic religion, *both* sides face difficult questions. The advocate of religion must face Marx's charge (religion is a
tool of class exploitation), Nietzsche's charge (God inhibits
vitality), Freud's charge (belief in an infantile illusion),
Dewey's charge (religion distracts us from social responsibility), Sartre's charge (faith is incompatible with freedom),
and the charge of third-world reformers that God is coun-
ter-revolutionary. The believer, moreover, must acknowledge a certain undeniable *bite* to these criticisms and a certain undeniable *nobility* in the humanism that inspires them.
The advocate of atheism, however, must also face charges:
Does the denial of God not finally undercut the atheists' affirmations? How can the total denial of God fail to deprive
human life of final meaning and ultimate worth, apart from
which (as Whitehead put it) the "insistent notion of right
and wrong, achievement and failure," human and inhuman,
authenticity and inauthenticity are "merely passing whiffs
of insignificance?"[35] Or, in the language of Pascal, when we
consider the briefness of ". . . life, swallowed up in the eternity before and behind, . . . engulfed in the infinity of spac-
es which [we] know not and which know not [us] . . ."[36] the

final meaning of life itself is in question, whatever its re-viseable conditions. What does it matter whether we creat-ed values freely or not, if life as a whole is finally meaning-less? How can the parts of the whole have meaning, if the whole is itself null and void? This is the dilemma of the hu-manism that typifies our age. It elevates humanity by what it affirms, but undercuts it by what it denies.

NOTES

1. I do not wish to suggest that Voltaire was unconcerned about evidence, and even less do I wish to suggest that Lord Russell was passionless. The story serves to dramatize ideal types.

2. All points are made by George Grant in his thought-provoking book from which I have learned much: *Time as History*, the Massey Lectures, ninth series (Toronto: Canadian Broadcasting Corpo-ration, 1969), 23 and 36f.

3. Ibid., 23.

4. Hans Küng, *Does God Exist? An Answer for Today*, trans. Edward Quinn (Garden City, New York: Doubleday and Company, 1978), 353.

5. Translated by Walter Kaufman, with *On the Genealogy of Morals* (New York: Vintage, 1967).

6. Friedrich Nietzsche, "At Noon," *Thus Spake Zarathustra* in: *The Portable Nietzsche*, ed. and trans. Walter Kaufman (New York: The Viking Press, 1954; Penguin ed., 1976), 387-389.

7. Any brief characterization of Hegel is going to be a gross oversimplification. Hegel's overall position is that the spirit, whether human or divine, comes to itself or constitutes and fulfills itself in the being of the other: the finite, individual spirit through the Absolute and the Absolute through the finite, individual spirits. This has some conti-nuity with medieval mysticism. I am indebted to Michael Welker for this insight.

8. See Ludwig Feuerbach, *The Essence of Christianity*, intro. Karl Barth, Hans George Elliot and foreward by H. R. Niebuhr (New York/London: Harper and Row, 1957), *passim*.

9. Ibid., 140-149.

10. Ibid., 33-43.

11. Ibid., 44-49.

12. Ibid., 50-59.

13. Ibid., 59-64.

14. Quoted from Feuerbach's *Das Wesen der Religion* by Karl

Barth, "Introductory Essay" in: Feuerbach, *Essence*, xi.

15. Friedrich Nietzsche, *The Will to Power*, trans. Walter Kaufman and R. J. Hollingdale, ed. with commentary, Walter Kaufman (New York: Random House, Vintage Books, 1968), Two, II, especially pp. 146-219. Feuerbach also specified a motive for the projection, a motive of a rather general sort. So we must say that Nietzsche added a new and more specific motive.

16. For the first appearance of Nietzsche's doctrine or thesis of the will to power, see *Zar.*, I, 15, 170-172. For the full elaboration, see Nietzsche, *W.P.*, 170-172, *passim*.

17. Friedrich Nietzsche, *On the Genealogy of Morals*, trans. Walter Kaufman and R. J. Hollingdale, with *Ecce Homo*, trans. Walter Kaufman (New York: Vintage, 1967, 1969), I, 24-57.

18. Nietzsche, *W. P.*, Two, II, 91. See also his *Genealogy*, III, 121ff

19. Ibid., Two, II, 213.

20. Ibid., Two, II, 207.

21. Ibid., Two, II, 254.

22. Ibid., Two, II, 145.

23. Ibid., Two, II, 145.

24. Ibid., Two, II, 146.

25. Friedrich Nietzsche, *The Gay Science*, trans. Walter Kaufman (New York: Vintage, 1974), IV, 279.

26. Ibid., aph. 125, 181.

27. Ibid., III, 181f.

28. Jean Paul Sartre, "Existentialism as a Humanism," trans. Philip Maret, in *Existentialism from Dostoevsky to Sartre*, ed. Walter Kaufman (New York: Meridian Books, Inc., 1957), 294.

29. Friedrich Nietzsche, *G.M.*, III, 163.

30. Nietzsche, *W.P.*, Three, I, 261-331.

31. Friedrich Nietzsche, *Beyond Good and Evil*, trans. Walter Kaufman (New York: Vintage, 1966), 17.

32. I agree here with Grant, *T.H.*, 44.

33. Austin Farrer, *The Freedom of the Will* (London: Adam and Charles Black, 1958, 1966), 299.

34. Farrer, *F.W.*, 299f.

35. Alfred North Whitehead, "Immortality," in *The Philosophy of Alfred North Whitehead*, ed. Paul Arthur Schilpp (New York: Tudor Publishing Co., 1941, 1951), 698.

36. Quoted in Stephen Toulmin, *An Examination of the Place of Reason in Ethics* (Cambridge: Cambridge University Press, 1950), 209f.

III

THE WILL TO POWER AND THE LOSS OF EXPERIENCE

Our starting point has been an observable fact, the fact that belief in God—indeed the very question of God—has grown dim in the Western world. Friedrich Nietzsche named this the "death of God."[1] More accurately, if less dramatically, Martin Buber named it "the eclipse of God."[2] It is a major mutation in the Western tradition, the consequences of which we are only now beginning to understand.

In the previous chapters two dominant modes of thinking and feeling in our society have been identified. We have noted the fate of the idea of God in each: in the first chapter I identified one mode as scientific objectivism, where belief in God has come to be regarded as cognitively dubious and in the second chapter another mode as humanistic subjectivism, where belief in God is rejected as oppressive and morally offensive.

There is an obvious sense in which these two modes are in tension with each other and are even antithetical. What I have called subjectivism reacts not only against perceived religious oppression, but also against the aridity of scientism. Consider, for example, 19th century Romanticism, Nietzsche's repudiation of scientific truth in favor of art, and counter-cultural phenomena in more recent times. There are those among us who believe that energy, imagination, and creativity—if only freed from the inhibiting demands of the intellect—would promote a flowering of humanity. When the results of such "liberation" are disappointing, if not vulgar, bizarre, or even brutal, there is an appeal for a "return to reason." Reason, when circumscribed by the norms of scientific rationality, however, seems too restrictive to include many things that matter to most of us, most notably aesthetic and moral concerns and questions of meaning. If reason will and can only deal with value-free facts, and if facts themselves are defined quite narrowly, then many people are prompted to abjure rationality altogether in dealing with non-scientific concerns in favor of one or more among the almost endless variety of irrational alternatives. And this then generates its opposition. So the cycle continues. The antithesis is clear as are its reasons for continuing.

However, beneath the *opposition* between objectivism and subjectivism, there is a more fundamental *inner affinity*. The *inner affinity* lies in their common orientation to the world. It is an orientation that may be described as managerial, willful, and dominating. This is a major thesis of this book.

Obviously it does not require much argument to convince a person that subjectivism is managerial and willful since, as we have seen, its chief representative, Friedrich Nietzsche, made, as we have observed, the will to power his first philosophical principle. It might seem quite implausible, however, to make the same case concerning scientific objectivism. For what is science but the unrelenting effort to put aside bias, subjectivity and willfulness in order to see things as they really are? Modern scientific thinking is so distinct in the popular mind from previous forms of thinking, that it has effected what John Dewey calls a "revolution in the seat of intellectual authority."

While there is no reason to deny either the novelty or success of modern science, critics are now astutely questioning the conventional image of it as an entirely disinterested, neutral, inductive, empirical endeavor. There is a partially underground discussion concerning the nature of rationality itself, which illustrates this questioning of science's conventional image. Some of the landmarks in this discussion permit and warrant attention here.

Let us turn first to the English-speaking discussion. In 1958, Peter Winch examined the nature of scientific explanation in *The Idea of a Social Science and its Relation to Philosophy*.[3] The most obvious point of the book was to warn social scientists of the difficulties and dangers involved in studying their subject matter when this subject matter is not inert material, but human subjects who happen to live in a different culture from that of the scientist. More pointedly, when we study a human subject, we study a person who constitutes, and is constituted by, a world of meanings and values; he or she is not simply an object to be explained in terms of the laws of nature. The trouble is, however, that the social scientist also lives in, and works out of, his or her own world of meanings and values, which are likely to be quite different from that of the people being studied. By arguing for these points, Winch—a student of the "later" Wittgenstein—is siding with and developing the position of Dilthey and Weber against the idea dominant in the English-speaking world since J. S. Mill that there are no logical or conceptual differences between studying nature and studying society.

The import of Winch's argument is twofold: it not only shows the differences between a subject matter of cultural subjects and natural objects but also serves to make the scientist understand his or her own acts of inquiry better. And his argument applies as well to the natural scientist as it does to the social scientist, when he contends that scientific inquiry occurs always within a conceptual framework that decides in advance what that science is to regard as real. As he puts it, the question as to "what is" cannot be "settled by experimental methods alone," for that question is not an empirical one at all but is conceptual.[4] "It cannot," writes Winch, "be answered by generalizing from particular instances, since a particular answer to (such a question) is already implied in the acceptance of those instances as "real."[5] The collection and study of data presuppose some prior agreement, even if only implicit, to a "rule," accord-

ing to which judgments concerning identity and difference
are to be made.[6] This is so because to study something is
"to identify relevant characteristics, which means that the
noticer must have some concept of such characteristics."[7]

In effect, then, Winch not only challenges Mill and
others by providing an astute defence of the distinction between what the Europeans call the *Geisteswissenschaften*
(social sciences and humanities) and the *Naturwissenschaf-
ten* (natural sciences), but also, in so doing, convincingly
demonstrates the importance of another continental insight,
often hitherto neglected in the English-speaking world,
namely, the role *a priori* factors play in human observation.

Whereas Winch speaks of shared rules, Thomas
Kuhn prefers to speak of paradigms, claiming that "paradigms can guide research even in the absence of rules."[8]
Kuhn's account of paradigms in *The Structure of Scientific
Revolutions*, virtually an epochmaking book, has been criti-
cized for not providing a clear, precise, and univocal definition of paradigm. However, the broad lines of his argument
are quite clear. Scientific research occurs within various traditions which are themselves energized, shaped, and guided
by dominant models or paradigms, and serve to generate
questions, define problems, and decide in advance on the
initial plausibility of various programs, projects, and hypotheses. A paradigm communicates to the scientific community what sort of information or evidence will count as a
fundamental explanation. It both opens up and restricts the
phenomenological field accessible for investigation, research, study, and testing.[9]

The *a priori* status of paradigms in Kuhn's account
is further made evident by his contention that paradigms
are never set aside simply by the discovery of anomalies or
"counter instances" which do not match expectations. A
paradigm rather is surrendered only when a scientific community is "converted," not by negative instances but, at
least in part, by the discovery of a superior paradigm. And
although conversions may be anticipated and although
there may be cumulative factors, they are themselves final-

ly best described in revolutionary, not evolutionary terms, as the very title of Kuhn's work suggests. Paradigm changes are characteristically vigorously championed and vigorously contested, involving as they do the radical restructuring of the corporate life and intellectual activities of the relevant scientific community.[10] For different paradigms vary not only in substance, but also in the "methods, problem-field, and standards of solution accepted by any mature scientific community at any given time."[11] Paradigm shifts are like gestalt-switches: "what were ducks in the scientists's world before the revolution are rabbits afterwards."[12]

Hence, adherents of newer and older paradigms have difficulty in debating or even understanding their differences, since a common framework is not readily available. Nor can the reasons for a paradigm-shift be easily stated or even identified. The reasons are not like mathematical or logical inference. There is no "neutral algorithm . . . no systematic decision procedure"[13] for choosing paradigms. Kuhn, anticipating criticism, denies in the book's postscript that paradigm shifts are totally arbitrary. But, for him, they cannot be said to be totally rational either. Kuhn avers that there is something like faith and religious commitment that inform paradigm shifts and choices.[14] Also, he says that paradigm shifts and choices include values reflecting such things as "aesthetic considerations."[15] He also speaks of the roles played by social, historical, and political considerations.

If Kuhn stops just short of portraying scientific reason as arbitrary, Paul Feyerabend in his *Against Method* does not.[16] Feyerabend, once closely aligned with Karl Popper, now attacks the "gang" of critical rationalists. He argues that science is an "irrational" enterprise, which indeed is at its best when its irrationality is uninhibited. Accordingly, Feyerabend now ridicules and seeks to undercut and subvert the "puritanical seriousness" of Popper and others.[17] (Richard Bernstein suggests a comparison of "the style and content" of Feyerabend's attack on contemporary scientific ideals of method and rationality, and "Jacques

Derrida's 'punning assaults' on the 'metaphysics of presence'."[18]

Feyerabend argues that the idea of science as a neutral, disinterested, and purely logical operation "is both unrealistic and pernicious."[19] It is unrealistic, for scientific "development" is anything but gradual and orderly: it occurs when scientists are free to abandon one way of structuring the world for another. It is "pernicious," because it is pretentious, concealing as it does the "ideolog[ical]" and myth[ical] basis of the way any given scientific community construes the world."[20] It thereby tempts a scientific community *to pretend* "greater authority" than "other form(s) of life."[21] Feyerabend say that the myth of pure science and disinterested method camouflages the dependence of science on "culture, ideology, [and] prejudice."[22] It disguises the fact that science is frequently guided "by non-scientific influences,"[23] i.e., that it is an "historical phenomenon."[24] The idea that science provides the only approach to a problem, or even that it is an especially privileged approach, is "but another and most convenient fairy-tale."[25]

By now, it will have become obvious that Feyerabend is a more radical thinker than even Kuhn, and it may very well be that Feyerabend exaggerates the subjective factors at play in the practice of science. But at the very least, what Kuhn, Feyerabend and Winch agree on—and this they do very much for the same reasons—is the inadequacy of the orthodox empiricist account of scientific work.

I now propose that we consider Mary Hesse, a distinguished but more sober and cautious philosopher of science than either Kuhn or Feyerabend. In so doing, we will note that, though her tone is measured, her message is strikingly supportive of the common position already emerging, i.e., that pre-systematic factors enter into science as it is practiced today.[26]

Moreover, Hesse shows something else of extraordinarily great interest, namely, the similarities between the new accounts of science in English-speaking philosophy of science, e.g., Kuhn, Feyerabend, *et.al.*, and contemporary

Continental hermeneutic philosophy. The argument has its ironies. Whereas we are accustomed to seeing the contrast between the natural sciences and social sciences (*Natur/Geisteswissenschaften*) attacked from the side of those who recognize the validity of only the former, Hesse criticises the distinction from the other side. She supports her position by first summarizing in five points the usual distinctions made in Continental philosophy between the natural and social sciences (as found, for example, in Jürgen Habermas's *Knowledge and Human Interests*).[27]

> 1. In natural science experience is taken to be objective, testable, and independent of theoretical explanation. In human science data are not detachable from theory, for what count as data are determined in the light of some theoretical interpretation, and the facts themselves have to be constructed in the light of interpretation.
> 2. In natural science theories are artificial constructions or models, yielding explanation in the sense of a logic of hypothetico-deduction: if external nature were of such a kind, then data and experience would be as we find them. In human science theories are mimetic reconstructions of the facts themselves, and the criterion of a good theory is understanding of meanings and intentions rather than deductive explanation.
> 3. In natural science the law-like relations asserted of experience are external, both to the objects connected and to the investigator, since they are merely correlational. In human science the relations asserted are internal, both because the objects studied are essentially constituted by their interrelations with one another, and also because the relations are mental, in the sense of being created by human categories of understanding recognized (or imposed?) by the investigator.
> 4. The language of natural science is exact, formalizable, and literal; therefore meanings are univocal, and a problem of meaning arises only in the application of universal categories to particulars. The language of human science is irreducibly equivocal and continually adapts itself

to particulars.
5. Meanings in natural science are separate from
facts. Meanings in human science are what constitute facts, for data consist of documents, in-
scriptions, intentional behaviour, social rules,
human artifacts, and the like, and these are in-
separable from their meanings for agents.[28]

Hesse proceeds to argue that the account of natural
science at work in this contrast is quite passé, presupposing
as it does "a traditional empiricist view of natural science
[that is now] almost universally discredited."[29] As a matter
of fact, Hesse contends, almost every point in the above di-
chotomy (i.e., in effect Habermas's account of the matter)
characterizing the human sciences has recently been made
in current Anglo-American philosophy of science about the
natural sciences.[30] In sum, the "traditional empiricist view"
of natural science held

that the sole basis of scientific knowledge is the
given in experience, that descriptions of this
given are available in a theory-independent and
stable language, whether of sense-data or of
common-sense observation, that theories make
no ontological claims about the real world in so
far as they are reducible to observables, and that
causality is reducible to mere external correla-
tions of observables.

But current philosophy of science, explains Hesse, simply
does not accept this as an apt description.[31] On the contrary,
Wittgenstein, Quine, Kuhn, Feyerabend, and others, she re-
ports, have convincingly shown that "the descriptive language of observables is 'theory-laden'," which is to say,
that we grasp data interpretatively, in terms of "some general view of the world."[32]

Keeping in mind Hesse's previously quoted account
of the human sciences, let us now take note of her characterization of the understanding of science to be found in the
most recent English-speaking philosophy of science:

1. In natural science data is not detachable from theory, for what count as data are determined in the light of some theoretical interpretation, and the facts themselves have to be reconstructed in the light of interpretation.

2. In natural science theories are not models externally compared to nature in a hypothetico-deductive schema, they are the way the facts themselves are seen.

3. In natural science the law-like relations asserted of experience are internal, because what count as facts are constituted by what the theory says about their interrelations with one another.

4. The language of natural science is irreducibly metaphorical and inexact, and formalizable only at the cost of distortion of the historical dynamics of scientific development and of the imaginative constructions in terms of which nature is interpreted by science.

5. Meanings in natural science are determined by theory; they are understood by theoretical coherence rather than by correspondence with facts.[33]

One can readily see from this that the so-called "hermeneutical-circle" which is operative in the human sciences is hardly less operative in the natural sciences. In both, data are always given an interpretation; they are apprehended and construed in light of some prior understanding of the whole. (This does not at all deny that the projected whole is constrained and sometimes modified by empirical study of the parts.) In both accounts there is a recognition of an *a priori* factor operative in human knowing. That factor is not an abstract transcendental or colorless invariant structure of pure reason; it is rather an anticipated totality shaped by a concrete "interest."[34]

Now I propose to tackle the same set of issues from, as it were, the other side of the English Channel. While I wish in no way to detract from the originality, integrity, and importance of the discussion on rationality now occurring in the Anglo-American world of philosophy of science, I do think it is arresting and illuminating to observe that this discussion was anticipated in significant ways several decades ago on the Continent by the German philosopher Martin Heidegger.[35] This is striking for at least two reasons. First, we are accustomed to think of English and German-speaking (especially Heideggerian) philosophy as living in very different "worlds." And, second, Heidegger was not a philosopher of science. But he was one who thought about the question of Being and its self-manifestation in the inter-action between human beings and the world, an interaction which led him to reflect on human involvement in science and technology.

In *Being and Time (Sein und Zeit*, 1927), Heidegger argues that "a science's level of development is determined by the extent to which it is capable of a crisis in its basic concepts."[36] He observes that a crisis of this sort, occurred in and around the 17th century, which we recognize as the era conventionally identified with "the Scientific Revolu-tion" and "the dawn of the modern age." In a series of lec-tures later published as *What is a Thing?* (1935-36)[37] Hei-degger reflects on this crisis and the conceptual change that he believes defined that era (and subsequently our own). In seeking to distinguish ancient and medieval science from modern science, Heidegger rejects the popular belief that the former was content with mere concepts while the latter attends to facts. He understands this comparison to be sim-plistic, for concepts and facts come into play in both cases. Both ways of doing science are experimental. Their differ-ence lies in the different ways of setting up the experi-ments. These ways are determined, according to Heidegger, by differing "mathematical projections." Heidegger uses "mathematical" here in the first instance in the sense of the Greek word *"mathemata,"* a word whose meaning is not limited to the numerical. Its original meaning, rather, is "that about things which we really already know,"[8] in other words, it means a pre-understanding with which we ap-proach that which we want to know. It is a "fundamental position we take toward" the things we wish to understand. It is "the fundamental condition for the proper possibility of knowing."[39] Naturally, what Heidegger understands by the *"mathemata"* is at the crux of a basic change in scientific understanding and procedure. We can grasp Heidegger's meaning better as we follow his contrast of Aristotle's *On the Heavens* to Newton's *Principia Mathematica* and Galileo's *Discourses*. First, consider Newton's *Law of Motion*, where the centerpiece of his work, the law of inertia, is explicated. The law says in effect that "every body" (*corpus omne*) left to itself moves uniformly in a straight line. Already with the first words, *"corpus omne,"* the break with Aristotle is apparent; whereas Aristotle recognized two types of bodies, the earthly and the celestial, Newton subsumes all bodies under one heading. Moreover, Aristotle and Newton saw motion differently. The former observed that just as bodies differ, so also do motions, for motion is determined by the nature of a body. Each body has its own natural place and strives toward that place. In somber contrast stands Newton's *"corpus omne,"* which recognizes no distinction between types of bodies, motions, or places is recognized. Motions are not "determined according to different natures, capacities and forces, or the elements of the body, but [vice versa]."[40] All changes or motions are "linked together and uniformly based on the new basic position expressed in the First Law and which we call mathematical."[41]

Of course, the basis for Newton's "advance" over Aristotle had been laid in Galileo's famous Piza Tower "free-fall" experiment. One may recall that Galileo attempted, by dropping two objects of unequal weight, to refute Aristotle's belief that heavier objects would fall faster than lighter ones, the motion of each being determined by different natures. What one may not recall, however, is that both sides claimed victory, for the bodies did not arrive simultaneously, even though the time difference between the impacts was brief. The Aristotleans used the difference to vindicate their theory; in contrast, Galileo and his followers claimed victory by minimizing the slight delay, attributing it to imperfect laboratory conditions. If the objects had been

thrown with equal force on an infinitely extended and fric-
tionless plane and in a perfect vacuum, they argued, then
the motion of the bodies would have been uniform and per-
petual. The fact that no one had ever seen such a remarkable plane, however, reinforced the Aristotlean's incredulity,
while the fact that the interval was so brief reinforced Galileo's confidence in his theory.[42]

Concerning this episode, Heidegger remarks that
"[b]oth Galileo and his opponents saw the same 'fact'...
[b]ut interpreted [it] differently...."[43] In other words, they
saw it in light of different "*mathemata*." Galileo's opponents followed Aristotle by adhering to an interpretative
model lifted from the ordinary, common-sense experience
of nature, where dislodged rocks crash down the mountain-
side, sparks fly upwards, wood floats, and clouds drift, all
doing so because it is their respective natures to do so. Galileo's model, however, was nowhere to be seen, except in
the mind. His ideal laboratory was, quite plainly, a mental
construct, a limiting concept. Now from this alone, it does
not follow either that Galileo erred, or that he improved
upon Aristotle. To construe the issues this way would be to
oversimplify. But there is no denying that there were important consequences attendant to the shift in thinking between
them. Galileo's procedure, by abstracting from the hetero-
geneity of nature, discovered "a uniformity of all bodies according to relations of space, time, and motion."[44] This
achievement made possible "a universal uniform measure
as an essential determinant of things, i.e., numerical measurement."[45] Thus Galileo's "*mathemata*," in the sense of
paradigm, allowed and, indeed, required the application of
mathematics, in the sense of numerical numbers, to the
study of nature. The formulation of this insight requires
care. Heidegger's position is not simply that modern science arose because mathematics was applied to nature.
Rather, he writes, "mathematics, and a particular kind of
mathematics, could come into play and had to come into
play as a consequence of [Galileo's, i.e., the modern] projection."[46] Two consequences of this were that (i) Newton

could develop the physics of *corpus omne* and (ii) consequently modern technology could come to be, with the ready application of mathematics to the study of nature.

Just as Heidegger challenges the textbook account of the relationship between modern science and modern mathematics, so also does he challenge the conventional account of the relationship between modern science and technology. It is not the case, according to Heidegger, that our technology arose after our science and consisted simply of applying modern science to practical problems. Rather, Heidegger argues that (a) before technology is an activity, (b) technology is a way of seeing things. Or, more adequately, it is a way of letting beings reveal themselves. Even more specifically, it is a way of grasping nature as a "standing-reserve," i.e., as material that we can calculate, dominate and thereby use. Moreover, this way of viewing things, informed as it is by an interest in mastering, preceded and controlled, rather than followed, the development of modern science.[47] In Heidegger's words: . . . [humankind's] ordering attitude and behaviour display themselves in the rise of modern physics as an exact science.[48] "Modern physics is not experimental physics because it applies apparatus to the questioning of nature;" Heidegger says rather the case is exactly the reverse.

That is, he explains:

> Physics, indeed already as pure theory, sets nature up to exhibit itself as a coherence of forces calculable in advance.
> . . . [It] orders its experiments precisely for the purpose of asking whether and how nature reports itself when set up in this way.[49]

Modern science, then, is far from being the cause of modern machine powered technology. It is rather the forerunner within which the technological orientation *already* holds sway.[50]

Modern science can apply modern mathematics to nature precisely because nature has already been so rendered that mathematics can be applied to it. This means, of course, that the unique features of natural beings have been minimized and the similarities in their features have been maximized. The viewing of nature in such a way as to emphasize the "uniformity of all bodies according to relations of space, time, and motion," to repeat, thus "makes possible . . . a universal uniform measure as an essential determinant of things, i.e., numerical measurement."[51] Plainly enough, such a mathematicization of nature serves well the modern world's technological interest in the measuring and mastering of nature.

Although the discussion of Heidegger's account of science and technology could be considerably extended with profit, we have already seen enough to perceive the remarkable parallels between his thought and the later and independent developments in Anglo-American philosophy of science. Heidegger anticipates the later thinkers by rejecting the orthodox or textbook account of empirical science according to which knowing is simply a matter of observing what is out there. And Heidegger undermines this account in much the same way as do Kuhn, Hesse, *et al.*: he emphasizes the role that the subject plays in setting up and conducting experiments and construing, interpreting, and judging data. Heidegger speaks of the *a priori* role of the *mathemata* in observation in much the same way as Kuhn and others now speak of the *a priori* function of paradigms.

In light of Heidegger's understanding of the role of the active subject in the unified project that is modern science and technology, it is interesting and not surprising that he finds in Descartes an appropriate philosophical explication of that project's meaning. He finds in Descartes a conceptualization of "the fundamental position toward what is and toward the way in which what is, as manifest as such . . . [in modern science and technology].[52] This conceptualization is possible, says Heidegger, precisely because "modern natural science, modern mathematics, and modern metaphysics sprang from the same root of the mathematical in the wider sense."[53]

Heidegger's reading of Descartes differs somewhat, however, from the conventional account, which Heidegger describes as at best a "bad novel."[54] The determining element in Descartes' thinking, contends Heidegger, *was not urbane, cool scepticism, but aggressive affirmation.* Descartes was in strenuous and singleminded pursuit of certainty, an existential certainty analogous to the theoretical certainty to be found in geometry. This is what prompted him to take the *ego cogito* as the privileged point of departure for his philosophy and as the chief sample of reality itself. Whereas previous thinkers had taken as their starting place "what offered itself" e.g., the external world of nature, church teachings and traditions, etc., Descartes did not.[55] The external world did not satisfy his quest for certainty, it did not provide the compelling self-evidence, for example, that accompanies mathematics. The *"ego cogito"* alone—or more precisely, the *"cogito me cogitare"*—could supply that sort of existential certainty. Hence, the thinking ego became for Descartes the first reality. This reality, and the clarity, distinctness, and self-evidence which it provided, became the yardstick by which all other claims to truth were to be measured.

Now it is customary to speak of Descartes as having initiated a "turn toward the subject" in Western consciousness. This interpretation is endorsed by Heidegger. But in addition to endorsing it, Heidegger deepens the ordinary understanding of the phrase. He shows that, with Descartes, the very meaning of subject and subjectivity remarkably changes. "*Subjectum*," observes Heidegger, is the translation of the Greek "*hypokeimenon*": a word which names "that-which-lies before, which as ground, gathers everything unto itself."[56] Until Descartes, things in the world with which we have to do were "subjects." When the ego "becomes the primary and only real subjectum," however, this means that it "becomes that being upon which all that is, is grounded as regards the manner of its Being and its truth. [It] becomes the relational center of that which is as such."[57]

Furthermore, with the shift in the meaning of "subjectum," there occurs a corresponding shift in the meaning of "objectum." Prior to Descartes, "objectum" referred, says Heidegger, only to that which "was thrown up opposite one's mere imagining....[58] That is, it referred to what we would now call "merely subjective." It required still to be seen whether it corresponded with that "which-lies before . . . [and] gathers everything unto itself"—i.e., with the *subjectum* in the previously explained, earlier sense.[59] Now Descartes did not challenge this requirement, except that the "*subjectum*" became for him the "*ego cogito*." In a word, according to Descartes, beings become objects insofar as they are brought into a relation to the human knower i.e., insofar as they are constituted by the human subject.[60] The "beginning of beings" is defined thereby as "mere representation" or object-ness for the representing or "objectifying" ego.[61]

This "Copernican Revolution" in our interaction with the world allows us to attain in our own selves the security that was once sought through trust in God and trust in the world as God's creation. We will become "master(s) of [our] own surety and [achieve] certitude on [our] own terms."[62] The ego in possession of itself can proceed to possess its world insofar as the beings in the world can be objectified and thereby brought under control. In fact, only that which can be so objectified and mastered will be counted as real and true. In order to exercise this lordship over all things, what is required is a "method," a method so reliable as to yield certain results even if the universe were the creation of an "evil demon." "Method" is now "the name for the securing, conquering proceeding against beings, in order to capture them as objects for the subject," writes Heidegger.[63] The Cartesian method, as is well known, consists of the reduction of all phenomena to units sufficiently small and discreet as to permit their subsumption under mathematical procedures whose basic principles can be taken as self-evident. On this basis and proceeding cautiously step by step, Descartes' famous methodology promises to enable the human subject to construct a world of certain knowledge.

If Heidegger finds Descartes to represent philosophically the meaning of modern science and technology, this is not all that he finds. In 1961 Heidegger published a massive Nietzsche study (the substance of which was given in the 1940's as lectures in the University of Freiburg), whose central intention was to show a connection between Nietzsche and Descartes.[64] The connection for which Heidegger argues, is not so much one of historical dependence, but more one of philosophical affinity. "Nietzsche stands," writes Heidegger, "on the ground of metaphysics laid out by Descartes."[65] By this he does not mean shared conclusions, for Nietzsche obviously differed with Descartes consistently in this regard. Nietzsche does however follow Descartes' turn toward the *human* subject as providing a foundation and point of departure for thinking. Nietzsche agrees with Descartes in finding in the human subject that reality which gathers all else unto itself. Moreover he agrees with Descartes that the beings of things is constituted by their being "represented" and "established" in the thinking of that subject.

Nietzsche does not, however, agree that with the *ego cogito* rock bottom has been reached, for he believes that even deeper than the thinking of the subject is the will to power. It will be recalled from the previous chapter, that Nietzsche goes so far as to find the will to power at the heart of everything. What gives special plausibility to his thesis in this instance, however, is Descartes' self-acknowledged "quest for unshakeable certitude," his unwillingness to risk error or to rely upon tradition or revelation to avoid it, and his desire to bring all under this control.[66] Nietzsche renders Descartes' *"ego cogito"* as *"ego volo"* and then "interprets the *velle* as willing in the sense of will to power."[67] For Nietzsche, "the principle ego cogito" ergo sum is only an "hypothesis," assumed by Descartes because it gave him the greatest feeling of power and security.[68] And Nietzsche thought he was agreeing with

Descartes in interpreting "Truth" and "Being" to mean that
which can be secured, ordered, and mastered.[69] Nietzsche
claimed that for Descartes logic was nothing transcendental; it was but a way of positing and ordering phenomena,
an instrument of the will to master.

In brief, Heidegger sees in Descartes and Nietzsche
a common turn to the subject as the organizing center of all
things. Whereas Descartes, however, stopped at reducing
all things to the realm of the ego's representations and consciousness, Nietzsche reduced the ego itself to the realm of
appetites, drives and ambitions in the service of the will to
power.

In conclusion, let us observe that we began with an
opposition between two movements in our culture. On the
one hand, there was scientific objectivism: proud, sovereign, disinterested, omnicompetent, and value-free. On the
other hand, there was subjectivism: restless, vital, but rud-
derless and empty. In this chapter, however, resources have
been found for changing the situation in both recent Anglo-
saxon philosophy of science and in the writings of the German, Heidegger. For they have argued in different ways for
a different understanding of the modern scientific method.
They have, in short, revealed it to be a project informed by
human interests and purposes.

But have they opened the door to cognitive nihi-
lism, i.e., a science that is also "truth-free," as it were? Feyerabend comes close to this as does Nietzsche. This is not,
however, the common position of Winch, Kuhn, Hesse and
Heidegger.

For example, Winch explicitly cautions that "[w]e
should not lose sight of the fact that the idea that [our] ideas
and beliefs must be checkable by reference to something independent—some reality—is an important one."[70] Similarly
Kuhn warns that it does not follow from the fact that "two
groups of scientists see different things when they look
from the same point in the same direction," that "they can
see anything they please. Both are looking at the world."[71]
And Hesse strives to show that, while "post-empiricist"

philosophy of science allows us to see that science emphasizes "instrumental control rather than with theoretical discovery, the claim to objectivity can still be defended."[72]

As for Heidegger, while he argues that a technological interest is at the base of modern science, he also argues that technology is no mere means to an end but is itself "a way of revealing."[73]

On the one hand, therefore, the post-empiricist philosophers of science and Heidegger allow that though our view of the universal is not itself universal, they insist that it is nevertheless a view of the universal (to use H. R. Niebuhr's lapidary formulation).[74] In other words, they are not subjective idealists or, as I call them, "cognitive nihilists."

On the other hand, they do give us a different view of modern science and its methodology from the one to which we are accustomed. What we have instead is a science that is anything but value-free. More specifically what we have is a science that is rooted in and expressive of certain interests. And these interests and the truth that they allow to appear are products of a certain way of being-in-the world.

Is this a more modest view of science? Surely the answer is both yes and no. The answer is yes, in the sense that we have experienced the dethroning of the idea of science as the impartial, disinterested, and sovereign account of "the truth, the whole truth, and nothing but the truth," to borrow courtroom language. Its pretense to be an innocent and neutral "superlook" at (in Lonergan's phrase) the "already-out-there-now real" has been exposed.[75] We now see that science is a freely chosen standpoint or project. "Within our own 'post-modern' world," as Stephen Toulmin observes, "the past scientist's traditional posture as *theoros*, as spectator, can no longer be maintained: we are always— and inescapably—participants or agents as well."[76] We have in our time witnessed the "death of the spectator (image) of the modern scientist."[77]

But the answer is no, this is not a more modest view in the sense that the special interest which modern science serves is anything but a humble one. Hesse writes, for example, that our scientific theories are permeated by our own "self-understanding." Nor is this, she adds, simply to say that human values "will be involved in applications of these theories, though that is true too; it is also . . . to assert that the very categories of these theories . . . are infected by [our] view of himself [ourselves]." And that view, she states, is of one who exercises technical control.[78]

Finally, we may notice a paradox: the more we have been able to make an object out of nature, the more we have been able to exercise our own will, that is, our subjectivity, on nature. And with the resulting technology, we have been able to move into a lordlike position vis à vis our environment. Nor are the benefits of this to be cheaply denied. But, as with the case of Prometheus, our achievement comes with a price. For one thing, though nature may now be largely at our disposal, it is no longer experienced as our home. Wordsworth speaks for us all: "Little we see in Nature that is ours. It moves us not—Great God!" Though we may now be able "[to] put her on the rack to compel her to answer our questions," as Bacon predicted we would, nature is no longer experienced as our friend.[79]

Whether to proceed with modern science and technology is hardly a real question for us, for they have become our destiny. The human will has had a large part to play in the genesis of the technological age, but once here this age certainly can not be willed away. Nor is it clear that we would want to escape this age, even if we could. For it can be argued that learning to exercise dominion over the earth is part of humanity's coming of age, a legitimate form of self-development. Taken by itself, however, our present, dominant orientation is constricting and debilitating. Martin Buber is at least partially successful in saying why:

> ... the I-it relation . . . has usurped...the mastery
> and the rule. The I of this relation, an I that pos-
> sesses all, makes all, succeeds with all, this I
> that is unable to say thou . . . is the lord of the
> hour. This selfhood that has become omnipo-
> tent, with all the It around it, can naturally ac-

knowledge neither God nor any genuine absolute which manifests itself to [us] as of non-
human origin. It steps in between and shuts off
from us the light of heaven.[80]

The managerial orientation, common to scientific objectivism and humanistic subjectivism, does not of itself render us open to the Eternal or Transcendent. It is a posture of control, pride, and aggression, not contemplation, trust, and adoration. And to the extent that it moves from being a useful part of our lives to being the whole of our existence, there will surely be consequences at odds with the heart of the religious vision of life.

NOTES

1. Friedrich Nietzsche, *The Gay Science*, trans. Walter Kaufman (New York: Vintage, 1974), III, 125, 181f.

2. Martin Buber, *The Eclipse of God: Studies in the Relation Between Religion and Philosophy* (New York: Harper and Bros., 1957).

3. Peter Winch, *The Idea of a Social Science and its Relation to Philosophy* (London: Routledge and Kegan Paul, 1958, 1970).

4. Ibid., 7.

5. Ibid., 9. Parenthesis added.

6. Ibid., 84.

7. Ibid., 85.

8.Thomas S. Kuhn, *The Structure of Scientific Revolutions* (Chicago: University of Chicago Press, 1962, 1970), 42.

9. Ibid., 41-62.

10. Ibid., 94.

11. Ibid., 103.

12. Ibid., 111.

13. Ibid., 200.

14. Ibid., 158.

15. Ibid ., 92-110.

16. Paul Feyerabend, *Against Method: Outline of an Anarchistic Theory of Knowledge* (London: Verso, 1975, 1982).

17. Richard J. Bernstein, *Beyond Objectivism and Relativism: Science, Hermeneutics and Praxis* (Philadelphia: University of Pennsylvania Press, 1985), p. 4.

18. Ibid., 18.

19. Feyerabend, *Against Method*, 295.
20. Ibid., 299.
21. Ibid.
22. Ibid., 302.
23. Ibid.
24. Ibid., 308.
25. Ibid., 306.
26. Mary Hesse, "In Defence of Objectivity," in: *Proceedings of the British Academy*, 57 (London: Oxford University Press, 1973), 275-292. See also Hesse, *Models and Analogies in Science* (Notre Dame, Indiana: University of Notre Dame Press, 1970), passim and Michael A. Arbib and Mary B. Hesse, *The Construction of Reality* (Cambridge: Cambridge University Press, 1986), Chapters 7-9.
27. Jürgen Habermas, *Knowledge and Human Interests,* trans. Jeremy J. Shapiro (Boston: Beacon Press, 1971), passim.
28. Hesse, "Objectivity" (in PBA), 277-278.
29. Ibid., 279.
30. Ibid.
31. Ibid.
32. Ibid., 280.
33. Ibid.
34. It is interesting that so much of this discussion of what constitutes fact and the relationship between fact and interpretation was anticipated in large measure by Alfred North Whitehead. Whitehead, who was as much at home in mathematics and science as in philosophy, argued with great subtlety against the idea of bare, discreet fact that could be known apart from networks of relationships and systems of thought. His *magnum opus* remains *Process and Reality: As Essay in Cosmology* (New York: Macmillan; Cambridge, England: Cambridge University Press, 1929, 1960). Among Whitehead's many other works see *Science and the Modern World* (Cambridge: Cambridge University Press, 1938). It is strange that Whitehead is referred to so seldomly in the current English-speaking discussion.
35. Martin Heidegger, "The Question Concerning Technology," in: *The Question Concerning Technology and other Essays*, trans. with an introduction by William Lovitt (New York: Harper and Row, 1977), 3-36. This essay is based on Heidegger's 1949-50 Freiburg lectures.
36. Martin Heidegger, *Being and Time*, trans. John Macquarrie and Edward Robinson (New York: Harper and Row, 1962), 9.
37. Martin Heidegger, *What Is a Thing?*, trans. W. B. Barton, Jr. and Vera Deutsch (South Bend, Indiana: Regnery-Gateway, Inc, 1967).
38. Ibid., 74.
39. Ibid., 75.
40. Ibid., 87.

41. Ibid., 88.
42. Ibid., 88-95.
43. Ibid., 93.
44. Ibid.
45. Ibid.
46. Ibid.
47. Heidegger, *Question*, passim.
48. Ibid., 21.
49. Ibid.
50. Ibid., 22.
51. Ibid., 93.
52. Heidegger, *Thing?*, 96.
53. Ibid., 97.
54. Ibid., 99.
55. Ibid., 107.
56. Martin Heidegger, "The Age of the World Picture," in *The Question Concerning Technology and Other Essays*, op.cit., 128.
57. Heidegger, *Question*, 128.
58. Heidegger, *Thing?*, 105.
59. Heidegger, *Question*, 128.
60. Martin Heidegger, *Nietzsche*, IV, trans. Frank A Capussi; ed. David F. Krell (San Francisco: Harper and Row, 1982), 119.
61. Ibid., 119.
62. Ibid., 119f.
63. Ibid., 120.
64. Heidegger, *Nietzsche* (Pfullingen: Günther Neske Verlag, 1961). The English translation, which appeared in 1982, is cited above. Subsequent reference will be to it.
65. Ibid., 123.
66. Ibid., 129.
67. Ibid.
68. From Nietzsche's *Der Wille zur Macht*, aphorism no. 533. Quoted by Heidegger, Nietzsche, 131.
69. Ibid., 131.
70. Winch, "Understanding," 11.
71. Kuhn, *Structure*, 150.
72. Hesse, "Objectivity," passim.
73. Heidegger, "Question," 12.
74. H. Richard Niebuhr, *The Meaning of Revelation*, (New York: The Macmillan Company, 1960), 18.
75. Bernard F. J. Lonergan, *Insight: A Study of Human Understanding* (New York: Philosophical Library; London: Longmans, Green and Company, 1957), 251.
76. Stephen Toulmin, *The Return to Cosmology: Postmodern Science and the Theology of Nature*, (Berkeley, CA: University of California Press, 1982), 255.

77. Ibid., 237-254. Parentheses added.

78. Hesse, "Objectivity," 292.

79. William Barrett, *Death of the Soul: From Descartes to the Computer*, (New York: Anchor Press, Doubleday, 1986), 74. See also by the same author, *The Illusion of Technique: A Search for Meaning in Technological Civilization*, (New York: Anchor Press, Doubleday, 1978), 182.

80. Martin Buber, *Eclipse*, 162.

IV

THE RECOVERY OF EXPERIENCE
AND THE OPENNESS TO GOD

A great poet encourages us in saying, "When the danger grows, so also does the possibility of salvation."[1] Our chief danger, even greater and more fundamental than the still present danger of violence and war, is the continually tightening grip on our lives, individually and collectively, of technology and technological reason. While no one needs to break a lance defending the utility of technology, what we sense is that we ourselves are becoming the servants of our servant. While no one needs to insist on the capacity of scientific, technological reason to discover important truths, what we are increasingly coming to doubt is whether it can tell us all the truth we need to know. The dawning of the "possibility of salvation" may well be represented by the very fact that little by little we are growing aware of the insufficiency of this technological, managerial orientation. As instances of this awareness, we can advert not only to the phenomena of counter-cultural movements since the 1960's, but also to the scientific community's discoveries of the limitations of its own resources. Consider Gödel's incompleteness theorem, Polanyi's discovery of the "tacit dimension" presupposed by "focal knowledge," and the discovery in physics of the complex and unavoidable interaction of the observer and the observed in even the purest observations.[2] Kuhn's work, as well as that of Feyerabend and of Mary Hesse, has uncovered the role of values and human interests in the determination of even the barest

fact (as we saw in Chapter III above). We could also call to
mind Whitehead's break with Russell and his search for
broader modes of thought after the spectacular achievements of the monumental work, *Principia Mathamatica*,
and Wittgenstein's discovery that the rationality of his celebrated *Tractatus* does not displace but actually requires the
mediation of ordinary language.

   Modern Western humanity will not easily surrender
the hard-won achievements of the Enlightenment and of
modernity, e.g., the healthy distrust of truth-claims that cannot be guaranteed by experience. But we are witnessing a
new openness to the understanding of experience. If, for
convenience's sake, we may refer to the dominant understanding of the past 300 years, represented by Locke,
Hume, Moore, Ayer, and Flew as "classical empiricism,"
we may then place the newer understandings of experience
under William James' rubric "radical empiricism." I use the
term here even more widely than James did, including under it not only Dilthey, Bergson, and the American pragma-
tists, but also Whitehead, Heidegger, and the recent school
of hermeneutical philosophy. Whereas classical empiricism
equates experience and pure sense-perception, radical empiricism understands sense-perception to be neither the *only*
nor even the *basic* form of experience. Rather it takes sense
perception to be a derived mode of experience, deriving
from a more comprehensive and primary awareness of ourselves in interaction with our environing world. Before we
discriminate between ourselves as subjects and the world as
an aggregate of objects given to us as *sensa*, we are already
experiencing ourselves as acting, acted-upon, and interacting selves among other selves in a common world. Experience is richer, thicker, more complex and dynamic than traditional accounts of experience as mere sensation and pure
perception would have us believe. Among the many representatives of radical empiricism whose work would be
worth studying, I think especially of the American pragma-
tists, Whitehead, and even of the later Wittgenstein and,
more recently, of Bernard Lonergan. Here, however, I shall

discuss only one current: the hermeneutic theory of Hans-Georg Gadamer (as augmented by Bernard Lonergan).

Gadamer's thought begins with the discovery of the linguisticality of the world. In this regard he learned from both Husserl and Heidegger. Heidegger taught him to challenge the notion of pure facticity. Pure fact, Heidegger convincingly argued, is meaningless; the meaning of fact is dependent upon context. For example, apart from interpretation, data from the past are neither significant nor even intelligible; they remain *bruta facta*, brute or raw givens. Nor are *bruta facta* adequate for the experimental sciences. The idea that science, or any other human engagement with the world, could begin with innocent, disinterested, pure perception of bare facts or discreet sense data is a myth, for all encounters are mediated by some sort of interests, concerns, or practical involvements with things. Again, Edmund Husserl had earlier mounted an attempt to widen the scope of philosophical awareness beyond scientific activity to include *the sphere of ordinary experience*, the *Lebenswelt* or "life-world." Insight into the "life-world" revealed the managerial orientation to be only one of many forms of human interaction with the world and scientific knowledge to be inexhaustive of our multiple forms of perception and interpretation.

This legacy from Husserl and Heidegger was immensely helpful to Gadamer. It freed him from trying to understand the humanities solely on the model of the objectifying sciences; it also enabled him to resist the opposite tendency of dismissing or trivializing the humanities as "mere" subjectivity. It allowed him to understand truth as a mansion with many chambers, only one of which belongs to science. Art, poetry, morality, and religion also have their truth. Gadamer recognizes the legitimacy, dignity, and worth of objectifying science and the desire to control nature for certain purposes, but he challenges claims for scientific, technological hegemony. In the wake of Husserl and Heidegger, Gadamer seeks to reintegrate the scientific method back into the richly complex and varigated human world from which technology has abstracted it.

Gadamer emphasizes even more than his teachers, that our world is linguistically mediated. We have no extra-linguistic access to knowledge. Even mathematical signs which form systems intended to be unambiguously denotative, require the use of ordinary language for both their construction and application. Even the barest facts are directly or indirectly mediated by language.

Nor is language to be thought of as a storehouse of labels, rules, and recipes, isolated from concrete living and wholly at our disposal. No, "when you take a word in your mouth you have not taken up some arbitrary tool which can be thrown in a corner if it doesn't do the job, but you are committed to a line of thought that comes from afar and reaches on beyond you."[3] The language that mediates the world to us is the language of ordinary conversation; and our involvement with this language is not like the act of a technician using a tool, but like an *I encountering a thou.*

Gadamer finds the model for the I-thou encounter, however, in the Socratic dialogue, rather than in Martin Buber's well-known book. Although Gadamer agrees with Buber that the thou is more than the mere object which can be studied by the behavioral sciences, he stoutly denies that the encounter of I and thou is a sort of direct mystical communion between souls. The authentic encounter is a conversational affair. To acknowledge the other person's claim on us is to listen to what he or she has to say.

If Gadamer's view differs from Buber's, it differs even more from that of the American philosopher, Richard Rorty.[4] Rorty has followed Gadamer and the later Wittgenstein, among others, in overcoming false notions of objectivity and knowledge through the discovery of the role language plays in our understanding. But Rorty, I believe, fails to see what this involves. Conversation is not a matter of talking and then letting the other person talk. It is more demanding and rewarding than that. To listen to another calls for the complementary effort to understand what she or he means—and what it might mean for us, personally, if what the other means should be true. To listen is to keep ourselves open to the possibility that what the speaker is saying might modify our own life. To miss this is to run the risk of trivializing conversation.

For Rorty, overcoming the opposition between objectivism and subjectivism appears to lie in awarding the palm to subjectivism. The linguisticality of the world seems to mean that conversation can only be about more conversation. Gadamer, by contrast, does not allow mere conversation to replace real inquiry. The wheel of conversation on his account does not just spin, it rolls ahead, with its traction and power deriving from the skillful asking and answering of good questions.[5] This is how dialogue manages to enable someone to say something about something to someone. In the give-and-take, the to-and-fro of such living speech, truth comes to light.

Gadamer's accent on the dialectic of question-and-answer is indebted not only to his love of the Platonic dialogues but also to his reading of R. G. Collingwood, who influenced Lonergan as well. Collingwood, Gadamer, and Lonergan all reject the idea that the real comes to us already constituted and available. Lonergan's depreciatory tag for this is the myth of the "already-out-there-now-real." Its complement is the reduction of knowing to "taking a look." To this he opposes knowing as the cumulative sequence of experiencing, understanding, and judging.[6] Understanding answers a question, and answering questions presupposes the asking of questions: not idle but productive questions, questions that open things up, shed new light, and promote breakthroughs. Asking is an art and a discipline, as we learn from Collingwood, Gadamer, and Lonergan. We must be able to identify what we do not know, what it is we need to know, for as Plato's *Meno* shows, questioning presupposes a prior inkling of what one is inquiring into, and further inklings of how one might learn about it. Successful questioning depends upon following leads and finally, gaining insights. In the give-and-take of dialogue we must divine when to abandon a line of inquiry,

when to persist, and when it is possible to bolt through an
open door. All these unsystematic features of productive
questioning make clear why the hopes for an automatic,
omnicompetent, algorithmic method à la Descartes, Mill,
and modern technology must be scaled down. It is not possible to formulate rules for the asking of productive questions; and, if it were, we would still need to know how and
when to apply the rules (as Kant observed in his *Critique of
Judgment*).

There are no precise rules for a good conversation.
The most we can say is that the conversation partners must
learn to submit to a common question. We must learn to
sense or reconstruct the question which the partner's assertion is intended to answer. We cannot understand another's
assertions in isolation from our own questions. We cannot
assume too quickly, however, that the other person's questions are the same as our own. Every question has its sup-
positions. For me to understand another's question means
to understand his or her world. This means, not psycholo-
gizing the other, but listening *from* what the other person
says to what he or she means (Polanyi). It means trying to
find a commonality between that question, that world, and
my own. It is only in this way that I can come to understand
the other's assertions as meaningful, which is a prior condition for understanding/interpreting them as true or false.
Only in this way can conversation partners experience the
emergence of a truth that belongs to neither the one nor the
other, but simply is. This commonality Gadamer called the
"fusion of horizons."[7]

In this life, "fusion of horizons" is certainly no more
final than any one conversation. When it occurs, it opens up
a common horizon or frame of reference, which, for a while
at least, may prove to be a fruitful area of inquiry. It soon
becomes obvious, however, that no achieved understanding
of the world is universal; the conversation between those
who want to know is rekindled, the dialectic of question-
and answer is renewed. The quest for truth may also be
squelched or sidetracked. For Heidegger, the key example

of inauthenticity was irresoluteness in the face of death; for Gadamer it tends to be infidelity to the demands of dialogue, the manipulating of conversation to a person's own ends, and the effort to unhorse an opponent rather than to collaborate with a partner. Fidelity to dialogue, and hence human authenticity, are attained through such self-denial in the sense of abandoning the fearful grasp after premature certainty, or sheer willfulness. To subordinate ourself to conversation may call for repentance (or the willingness to change) and faith (or trust in the direction that the dialogue naturally takes).

In the dialogical life, in addition to the dimension of strenuous demands, there is also a dimension of something like *grace*. Real conversation has a game-like or play-like character. This does not undermine seriousness and sincerity. But in the give-and-take of conversation, the participants, like players in a game, lose their self-consciousness. There is a sense in which the conversation takes over the participants, like a game playing itself out through the players. The rules of rational discourse, the grammar of language, and logical thinking remain in force, just as the rules of a game cannot be abandoned in the excitement. But the play of conversation is ecstatic, and the growing satisfaction, the shifts and occasional breakthroughs are *hardly dependent on strict adherence to rules*. Nor is the success or failure of conversation something that can be calculated or planned in advance.

We may say that we "conduct" a conversation, but in a truly sincere, engaging, and lively conversation, the conduct of the conversation transcends the will of the individual partners. We ourselves do not so much conduct a conversation as fall into it. In this vein, Gadamer writes that

> [t]o reach an understanding in a dialogue is not merely a matter of putting oneself forward and successfully asserting one's own point of view, but being transformed into a communion, in which we do not remain what we were.[8]

Gadamer compares the reciprocity, spontaneity, unpredictability, self-generating dynamics of living discourse to the play of a game, remarking that in the play, it is as true to say that the game plays us as to say that we play the game.[9] Moreover, "the 'because' disappears in play. Play is without a 'why.' It plays because it plays," as Gadamer's teacher Heidegger (following Meister Eckhart) expresses it.[10]

Now quite plainly this account of the dialogical structure of human experience challenges any and all notions of individual self-sufficiency and undercuts illusions of total technocratic management and control of life. This wider understanding of experience, of which Gadamer's hermeneutics is one among a number of instances, serves to remind us of a dimension of our existence upon which we all are dependent whether we recognize it or not. To be sure, we can and do fail to recognize it and also, we repress this recognition when it does occur. This is usually futile and self-contradictory behavior, but before such human ignorance or arrogance self-aborts, it tends to wreak havoc with the general ecology of life. The unchecked and unrestricted managerial orientation, even if in the service of individual liberation and fulfillment, is destructive of the very community which sustains it. It leads the individual, moreover, into a condition of emptiness and loneliness which renders him or her vulnerable to eruptions of self-pity, anxiety, aggression towards others, and finally self-destruction.

Perhaps the central figure of John Milton's *Paradise Lost* best symbolizes the situation of the managerial project. One will recall Lucifer's fall from being the angel of light to being Satan. In both of these states, Lucifer was ultimately and radically dependent upon powers outside of himself. The difference between his blessedness and damnation was that in the former state Lucifer acknowledged and accepted his dependence and in the latter state he did not.

If Gadamer helps us see the dialogical structure of our existence, he also helps us to recognize our dependence upon another reality. Conversation involves not only two (or more) conversation partners but also a shared horizon.

It is thus triangular. The shared horizon enables conversation partners to relate to one another meaningfully. They can discuss a table's relative solidity because both partners share the horizon of common sense; they can discuss it in terms of elastic repulsive forces, waves, particles and empty space if they share the horizon of theoretical physics. They can discuss the pros and cons of, for example, pacificism if they share the horizon of morality. But no horizon or fusion or merger of horizons, no attainment of a higher universality is a final achievement, for every horizon or whole, which we can achieve, attain, or even conceive, can be made into an object that can, in turn, be questioned. And every act of questioning, the ongoing life of dialogue, is a venture in quest for an ever yet more comprehensive and universal perspective, for the human spirit is capable of self-transcendence *ad infinitum*. Understanding is attained between dialogue partners, when a common horizon has been found. When dialogue partners are not content with their failure to understand each other, it is because there is a longing and hope to find a common horizon. Insofar as ignorance and bafflement are not accepted as the last word, it is because we trust that arbitrariness and absurdity are not at the heart of things, that things ultimately cohere, and that being is in itself intelligible, knowable, and worth knowing.

Obviously Gadamer's account of the human spirit as an irrepressible, spontaneous openness to an expanding, inexhaustable and universal horizon which engenders, supports, and eludes our acts of comprehending evokes religious interest. While it is not surprising that Gadamer, the philosopher, draws back from making theological assertions, it is also not surprising, that the theologian who believes on the basis of revelation that God is both the ground and goal, both the sustaining source and absolute future of us all will find in the philosophy of Gadamer (and other "radical empiricists") some indirect confirmation.[11]

Gadamer's philosophy also provides conceptual

models that are most helpful. For example, there is the model of the triadic structure of dialogue: dialogue partners in search of, or already sustained by, an encompassing horizon. The model of horizon and horizoned, or whole and parts, is one that is helpful in our search for more adequate ways of thinking and speaking of God.

For despite what a thoughtful believer knows, it is a common tendency to think of God as though God were, like ourselves though larger: hence, a being alongside other beings, a part of the whole of being rather than the whole itself. Perhaps it is not surprising that we do this, for practical considerations prompt us to attend more to variable parts of our environment rather than, say, the more nearly invariant environing whole itself, for there is less to be done about the latter. But, we can and often desire to avoid or control the former. To use an analogy, we can imagine that fish are more atuned to noticing other fish than the ocean itself. And to use another, we notice that physicists are more articulate in discussing the subject matter studied by physics than the nature of physics itself, for the physicist normally attends to matter and motion in light of the horizon of physics and less often to that horizon itself. There are, to repeat, practical reasons for this constriction of awareness, but it is a constriction nevertheless.

Similarly, religious people are prone to think and speak of God as though God were one being alongside of other beings. When this happens, people begin to suppose that belief in God is like a scientific hypothesis. This in turn prepares the way for scepticism and atheism, for as we saw in Chapter I belief in God cannot be formulated so as to meet the current scientific criteria for meaningfulness. It fails the test of empiricity, for the statement asserting divine existence does not make a prediction about a future state of affairs among a number of possible states of affairs which could be verified or falsified by future observations. God's reality, to the contrary, is not about a part of the whole; nor is it about one among several possible states-of-affairs. Rather it is about the ground and meaning of any and every conceivable state of affairs. Put differently, "God" is meant to refer to that invariant whole which encompasses every actual and possible being and occurrence. As the ancient council at Nicea put it, "God is the creator of all things visible and invisible." This does not mean that God may not prefer or will one state of affairs over another, but the theologian cannot be expected to specify a state of affairs, the occurrence or non-occurrence of which would be incompatible with the faith that God exists. The existence of God, the whole, unlike the parts of creation, is unobtrusive and is, in principle, compatible with any and every contingent possibility. The reality of God is believed to be, not contingently actual, but necessarily so.

Talk, however, of necessary reality is logically odd by contemporary standards for scientific discourse. This in turn raises the question as to whether talk of the whole, i.e., necessary existential truth-claims, are illegitimate or whether the regnant criteria for meaningfulness are too narrow. One of the considerations that gives plausibility to the latter possibility is the inability of the current criteria to validate themselves (Chapter I). To be sure, they can be validated on the grounds that their use enables us to master better the details of our environment. In light of the wider understanding of experience, however, it is hardly clear that this interest, whatever its validity in some instances, should become decisive in all.

Yet it is one thing to expose the arbitrariness and limits of one test for meaning and altogether something else to excogitate another, better one. If language about the whole is not to be vindicated as scientific or quasi-scientific, how may we speak? If the instrumentalistic language of prediction and control is unsuitable, what kind of language is suitable?

The perennial wisdom of religion would reply that the language of analogy and symbols is the appropriate language. But such language is dependent upon correct usage. Religious symbols are all too often misunderstood: they are taken not as symbolic references to the whole but as literal

stories referring to parts of the whole or to putative occur-
rences on the horizontal plane. For example the symbol of
creation becomes a report about a distant past event rather
than witness to the divine ground of all time. And the story
of Adam and Eve is taken to refer to an ancient couple rather than to our own predicament before God. Divine judgment and redemption are taken to be predictions about a
distant future event rather than a present reality.

When religious symbols are taken to be literal stories about intra-mundane events on a horizontal plane, they
lose their depth; they lose their power to illumine and transform. And they are easily discredited by natural science and
historical research. When, however, they are reoriented
from the parts to the whole and taken symbolically rather
than literally, the situation is quite different.

Skeptical questions, however, will still arise. Even
if it is admitted that an orientation to a whole or universal
horizon is constitutive of our dialogical existence, the question remains as to whether or not the anticipation is justified. Put differently, is human self-transcendence a trans-
cending towards transcendence or not (as the Marxist, Ernst
Bloch, asks in his *Atheismus im Christendom)?* [12] How do
we know whether the whole toward which we are oriented
is chaos, absurdity, nothingness or a real presence to which
or to whom religious symbols could somehow correspond?
Is the ultimate horizon nullity or Being? Believers and dis-
believers will differ here. As Leszek Kolakowski observes:

> To an earth-bound eye the religious mind is like
> Ixion copulating with clouds and breeding mon-
> sters. A denizen of the eternal, divinely super-
> vised order may say much the same of those
> who are deaf to the voice of God: they are at-
> tached only to what is shortlived and doomed to
> disappear in a moment; they are illusion hunt-
> ers, nothingness-seekers....[13]

How are we to decide in favor or against the affirmative case? Whereas followers of Vatican I will advocate
the proofs of natural theology, and followers of Karl Barth

will promote fideism, I incline to follow a less pure, middle way. Perhaps we might speak of a sort of "rational faith" or "soft-rationality," a mixture of faith and reason.[14]

The lines along which this way of thinking proceeds are as follows. If one does well to attend to the *difference* between whole and parts, as we did above, is it not also reasonable to see a *connection* between whole and parts? Is it not reasonable to assume that, while the whole can surely be much greater than the parts, it can be no less? Put differently, if and when *one* affirms one of the parts of the whole, *one* co-affirms the whole in the same measure.

Consider the dilemma of the nihilist who asks us to believe that the whole is null and void. Most of us would not subscribe to such a depressing hypothesis without the best of reasons. But how can the nihilist argue for the negative hypothesis without running into the contradictions of what Bernard Lonergan calls a self-reversing "counterposition," i.e., the advocacy of a hypothesis which is at odds with the performative act of advocating it; e.g., Hume arguing in a most original way that the mind cannot be original.[15] If *one* appeals to evidence, that is, appeals to rationality, intelligence, and good will in making the case that reality is itself illusory, absurd, null, void, or whatever, *one* is obviously in a highly paradoxical predicament at the very least. For as even Albert Camus confessed:

> From the moment one says that all is nonsense, one expresses something which has sense. Refusing all meaning to the world amounts to abolishing all value judgments. But to live, and, for instance, to take food is in itself a value judgment.... Anyway, what is the meaning of a literature of despair. Despair is silent.... A literature of despair is a contradiction in terms.[16]

We may also recall Nietzsche averring that rationality rests upon a metaphysical *faith* derived from Plato and the Bible, and that those who would break with that faith had not yet succeeded in doing so thoroughly and consistently and who: "are not yet good atheists for [they] still believe in grammar."[17] And we recall that Nietzsche also had trouble making his own, often astute arguments, apart from grammar (appeal to evidence, logic, etc.).

Such then are the difficulties in making the negative case. How is it with the positive case? Surely it cannot be proven in anything like a rigorous, self-sufficient, and "knock-down" manner, for the positive hypothesis is as much *presupposed* by the activity of reasoning as is the negative hypothesis contradicted by such activity. In other words, the very acts of attending to data, formulating hypotheses, listening to objections, and making rational judgments rest upon a confidence that reality is such as to warrant and reward such activity. It seems, then, that there is no neutral ground on which the rival hypotheses about the whole can be discussed.

Does this then mean that the choice between nihilism and its opposite can only be arbitrary? In a strictly formal sense, this may be the case. At an informal and existential level, however, there seems to be something in between the type of knockdown proof that one might get in mathematics (and aspire to in the hard sciences) and arbitrary choice.

The "soft-rationality" of this third, middle option can be seen by considering a variation of Dostoevsky's famous dictum "If there is no God, everything is permitted," namely: "If the Whole is null, all the parts are meaningless." If we consider the (paraphrased) dictum as a major premise, we can see that there are two ways of forcing from it a valid conclusion. In the minor premise, one may (1) affirm the antecedent ("The Whole is null") to get "all the parts are meaningless" in the conclusion (*modus ponens*). Alternatively, however, *one* may (2) deny the consequent in the minor premise ("Not all the parts are meaningless") and thereby in the conclusion validly deny that "The Whole is null" (*modus tollens*).[18] In other words, if *one* can affirm some part of the Whole as meaningful, *one* can deny the nihilistic account of the Whole itself.

The question, however, is whether we can affirm a

part of the whole nonarbitrarily. We can, I submit, insofar as we can unconditionally affirm as meaningful any of our own experiences or acts. If we can wholeheartedly affirm, for example, our own rational activity, we will have done this. In this case, the question would become: Is the affirmation of our rationality arbitrary or justified? It is arbitrary in the sense that there is no logical contradiction involved by not affirming it. We can simply lapse into silence, apathy, or despair. It may not be arbitrary, however, insofar as we may discover in the very act of being rational, meaning and satisfaction. We may find the act of being rational a fulfillment of our own deepest and most authentic nature as a person and essential to it.

The above is admittedly far from being a rigorous proof. For it may be objected that, on the major premise, one could not know that our rationality is meaningful unless we first knew that the Whole was meaningful, for the non-nullity of the Whole is the logical condition of the possibility of the existence of a meaningful part. The reply, however, will advert to the hermeneutical circle: we know the part by anticipating the Whole and the Whole by knowing the part. We have no unmediated knowledge of the Whole. We co-know the Whole in knowing the part. That is our only access to it.

We cannot know in advance, however, that the condition of the possibility of knowing is fulfilled, i.e., that the Whole is not null. So we must risk committing ourselves to rationality before we can know. In the act of being rational, however, we can come to know that the activity itself is meaningful. Or at least, insofar as we come to affirm that the effort to be rational is worth-while, etc., we co-affirm that the Whole is such as to warrant the effort.[19]

The same logic can be applied to moral experience. Insofar as we make a moral judgment and commit ourselves to moral action, we *eo ipso* co-affirm the non-nullity of the Whole. That is, we co-affirm a Whole in which such experience and activity make sense, i.e., are appropriate and justified.

Now an obvious objection to this line of argument is that it only succeeds in drawing a valid conclusion from a major premise that is itself quite dubious. Why, after all, should we make the meaningfulness of parts dependent upon the Whole, or more specifically, the meaningfulness of rationality and moral experience dependent upon something else?

In trying to respond to this objection, one will find it difficult to deny that much of everyday life is so immediate, routine, and, indeed, humdrum as to border on the involuntary. It may well seem implausible to suppose that the daily round is expressive of anything other than the natural vitality which George Santayana describes as "animal faith."[20] Perhaps "animal faith" is all we need most of the time.

In reply to this, can we not insist, however, that it is not all that we need all of the time? For our naive trust in our powers and our environment is inevitably called into question by the very nature of human existence: the workings of chance and the hard facts of suffering, transitoriness, loss of loved ones, and finally our own mortality. We cannot help then but wonder in the face of such crises, if our original, spontaneous confidence in life is at all warranted. In a word, while the question of the Whole may sometimes, even often, be avoidable, there are times when it clearly is not. As even Nietzsche, the opponent of theism, discovers:

> The world is deep,
> Deeper than day can comprehend.
> Deep is its woe, Joy-deeper than heart's agony:
> Woe says: Fade! Go!
> But all joy wants eternity, Wants deep, deep,
> deep eternity.[21]

The critic will object, however, that anguish over and longings for eternity in modern humanity's experience, if there be such, are mere failures of nerve—mere vestiges of a primitive heritage that has been rationally discredited but in practice, only partially left behind. They are testimonies only to a cultural lag. What, after all, was the Enlightenment, the critic will ask, but an effort to establish a rationality and a morality which are resolutely and uncompromisingly *autonomous?*

The argument for the Whole, however, neither opposes nor endorses without qualification the Enlightenment idea of autonomy. On the one hand, it does not favor heteronomous interference within the spheres proper to reason and morality. References to the Whole are no substitute for the functioning of human rationality—attentiveness to data, intelligence, reasonableness, and responsibility—within the horizons proper to the sciences and morality. Affirmations of the Whole are not gap-fillers for intra-mundane explanations. On the other hand, a philosophy of the Whole does deny the Enlightenment idea that human reasoning in these realms is *in every sense* self-sufficient and self-contained. On the contrary, reason itself is a thoroughly human affair, mediated by the interests and concerns of human community, and nourished by an anticipatory idea of the future. Sovereign mastery describes one role of reason, but fails to account for the totality of its human life. Reasoning, we have seen, rests upon a sort of trust and venture. The faith may not be justified. However, insofar as one trusts in reasoning, one trusts in the non-nullity of the Whole as the implied condition of reasoning's possibility.

Similarly, moral reasoning does not appeal to the Whole to relieve it of the task of determining which courses of action are best, i.e., most in keeping with the dignity of life. Moral reasoning itself, however, rests upon a trust that life has in fact such a dignity. As Stephen Toulmin puts it, "Ethics provides the *reasons* for choosing the 'right' course: religion helps us to put our *hearts* into it."[22] Implied in this is the recognition that we may in fact lose heart. We may know what the moral response in a given situation is, but we may waiver in our conviction that doing the moral thing is worth the trouble, risk, and sacrifice. In such instances, what we are asking for is reassurance that life itself is worth honoring. Or as Lonergan explains, moral experience calls for and opens the way to further development. For the moral person may well wonder if he or she is the terminal instance and source of moral concern—that is, a moral being in an amoral cosmos. Or are our moral efforts of a piece with a Whole that summons forth and supports our struggles for the good? For the theologian Lonergan, such wondering is a form of openness to divine grace, which is productive of ultimate "self-surrender without conditions, qualifications, reservations . . . a fated acceptance of a vocation to holiness."[23] An affirmative answer to this grace inspires a "total being-in-love as the efficacious ground of all self-transcendence, whether in pursuit of truth, or in the realization of . . . values, or in the orientation [one] adopts to the universe, its ground, and its goal."[24]

In sum, an affirmation of the meaningfulness of the Whole does not negate the spheres of scientific reason and morality but sublates them: i.e., transforms them by placing them in a more comprehensive and higher framework. Alternatively, one can say—following our paraphrase of Dostoevsky's dictum—that affirmations of human reason and morality are experiences which put us in contact with the Whole.

The Whole, however, is affirmed in many spheres of life other than those just discussed. Karl Rahner points to what he calls "anonymous" or implicit experiences of faith: e.g., acts of loving those who do not love us; forgiving even when one knows the act will be ignored or abused; sacrificing for others without expectation of thanks or recognition; enduring loneliness, disappointment, sorrow, and even death without either illusion or despair; and fighting for justice without bitterness or self-rightousness and without guarantee of reward or success.[25] Robert L. Calhoun and H. Richard Niebuhr speak of experiences of unconditional loyalty and reverence.[26] One also recalls Schleiermacher's references to the "feeling (*Gefühl*) of absolute dependence."[27] The mystics talk of experiencing a "consolation without an object,"[28] and Meister Eckhart bears witness to the experi-

ence of *"Gelassenheit"* and "unreserved gratitude."[29] Also
there is the feeling of an absolute protest against injustice:
experiences in which our sense of what is humanly permis-
sible is so fundamentally outraged that the only adequate
response to the offence . . . seems to be a curse of supernat-
ural dimensions.

What all of these experiences, for all of their obvious variety, have in common is reference to a sense of ulti-
macy sometimes encountered in the midst of ordinary living. They point to occasions in which human beings
occasionally experience the Whole, even if only implicitly
and anonymously, in interacting with the parts, and are able
to affirm that Whole as reliable and good.

Now I have not tried to prove that the Whole is in
fact reliable and good. I have tried to show that there is a
way to make such an affirmation; it is a way that, while certainly not rationally coersive or indubitable, is neither arbi-
tary nor fideistic. We can be true to it by being true to the
exigencies of our own rational and moral self-
consciousness. We cannot, however, find guarantees that
this act of fidelity is worthwhile before making the effort
and taking the risk it involves.

Nor have I argued that the Whole is, without further
ado, shown to be God. I personally believe that this is the
case. I recognize, however, that further argument would be
required to vindicate such a belief. And we would want to
consider very carefully other names and titles which people
from various traditions have used to speak of the Whole:
the Tao, Brahman, etc. My claim here is simply that a sense
of the Whole opens up a horizon within which talk of God
is at least meaningful and the question of God can become
real. Such sensing, thinking, and talking are not real so long
as one is bound by the calculative type of thinking that has
defined the technological age. If I have succeeded, however, in showing, or even making plausible the claim that
there is also another type of thinking, a meditative type of
thinking, a sort of musing that is open to and aware of the
Whole within which our living occurs, a significant step in

theological prolegomena will have been taken.

Such thinking is not entirely an achievement of the will, however, for it sets aside willfulness. It is not mere passivity either, for it requires attentiveness. It seems to be beyond the contrast of activity and passivity. It aspires to be an expansion of our consciousness of the ultimate environment within which we live. The Whole not being a part or an object eludes our words. To talk about it is to stammer and point to that ultimate mystery which nourishes (and mercifully limits) us in our doings and sufferings. Of course, we cannot speak about ultimate mystery with the clarity and precision that can be achieved when talking about things. Merely stammering about this mystery, however, is surely more important than speaking clearly about anything else.

NOTES

1. Martin Heidegger, "The Question Concerning Technology" in: *The Question Concerning Technology and Other Essays*, trans. and with intro. by William Lovitt (New York: Harper and Row Publishers, Torchbooks, 1977), 34. Heidegger is quoting Hölderlein.

2. Michael Polanyi, *Personal Knowledge: Towards a Post-Critical Philosophy* (New York and Evanston: Harper and Row, Publishers, 1958 and 1964), passim. For Gödel's theorem see Bernard Lonergan, *Insight: A Study of Human Understanding* (New York: Philosophical Library, 1957 and 1965), XXIV, XXV, and 574.

3. Hans Georg Gadamer, *Truth and Method*, 2nd, rev. ed., trans. revised by Joel Weinsheimer and Donald G. Marshall (New York: Crossroad, 1989), 269.

4. Richard Rorty, *Objectivity, Relativism, and Truth: Philosophical Papers*, Vol I (Cambridge: Cambridge University Press, 1991). See also Rorty, *Philosophy and the Mirror of Nature* (Princeton, N.J.: Princeton University Press, 1979).

5. Gadamer, *T.M.*, 341-380, esp. 369-380.

6. Lonergan, *Insight, passim*.

7. Gadamer, *T.M.*, 306-307, 374-375, 397, and 576. Michael Polanyi, *P.K., passim*.

8. Gadamer, *T.M.*, 379.

9. Gadamer, Ibid., 101-134 and esp. 104f.

10. Martin Heidegger, *The Principle of Reason*, trans. Reginald Lilly (Bloomington and Indianapolis, 1991), 41. See also his *Gelassenheit* (Pfullingen: Verlag Gunther, 1959). For commentary, see John Caputo, *The Mystical Element in Heidegger's Thought* (Athens, Ohio: Ohio University Press, 1977), *passim*.

11. Wolfhart Pannenberg, "Hermeneutic and Universal History in: *Basic Questions in Theology*, Vol. I (Philadelphia: Fortress Press, 1972), 129ff. See also Ted Peters, "Truth in History: Gadamer's Hermeneutics and Pannenberg's Apologetic Method" in *The Journal of Religion*, 55 (1975), 41ff.

12. Ernst Bloch, *Atheism in Christianity*, trans. J. T. Swann (New York: Crossroads, 1972).

13. Leszek Kolakowski, *Religion* (New York: Oxford University Press, 1982), 227.

14. I am in rough agreement with Hans Küng in finding a middle way between Vatican I and Karl Barth. See his, *Does God Exist?*, trans. Edward Quinn (New York: Random House, Vintage, 1981), 509-528.

15. Lonergan, *Insight*, 389.

16. Albert Camus, "The Riddle," *Atlantic Monthly* (June 1963), 85. Quoted in Schubert M. Ogden, *The Reality of God and Other Essays* (New York: Harper and Row Publishers, 2nd ed., 1977), 139f. Admittedly Camus did not conclude from this an explicit faith in the Whole or God. Ogden effectively criticizes his failure to develop his basic insight in this direction. See Ogden, *R.G.*, 41f.

17. Friedrich Nietzsche, *Twilight of the Idols* (Hammondsworth, N.Y.: Penguin, 1968), 38.

18. See the variations on Dostoevsky's dictum and brilliant and convincing critical and constructive responses to the issue of Ogden, *R.G.*, 128ff and Kolakowski, *Religion*, 82f.

19. Küng, *D.G.E?*, 509-551.

20. George Santayana, *Animal Faith and Spiritual Life*, ed. John Lachs (New York: Appleton-Century-Crofts, 1967), 23ff.

21. Nietzsche, *Thus Spoke Zarathustra*, trans. R. J. Hollindale (Hammondsworth, N.Y.: Penguin, 1961), 244. Nietzsche thematized this longed-for eternity in terms in "eternal recurrence of the same."

22. Stephen Toulmin, *An Examination of the Place of Reason in Ethics* (Cambridge: Cambridge University Press, 1961), 219. See Ogden's persuasive appropriation of Toulmin's concept of the limiting question in *R.G.*, 138ff. See David Tracy's theological appropriation of both Toulmin and Ogden in his *Blessed Rage for Order: The New Pluralism in Theology* (New York: Seabury Press, Crossroads, 1979), *passim*.

23. Bernard Lonergan, *Method in Theology* (New York: Herder and Herder, 1972), 240f.

24. Lonergan, *M.T.*, 241.

25. Karl Rahner, *Theological Investigations*, Vol. III: *Theology of the Spiritual Life* (New York: Seabury Press; London: Darton, Longman, and Todd, 1967), 86-89.

26. Robert L. Calhoun, *God and the Common Life* (New York: Charles Scribners and Sons, 1935 and 1954), 237-239. H. Richard Niebuhr, *Radical Monotheism and Western Culture* (New York: Harper and Row, 1960), *passim*.

27. F. D. E. Schleiermacher, *The Christian Faith*, eds. H. R. Macintosh and J. S. Stewart (Edinburgh: T. and T. Clark, 1928), 76-141 and also by Schleiermacher, *On Religion: Speeches to its Cultural Despisers*, trans. by John Oman (New York: Harper and Bros., 1958), 26-118.

28. Karl Rahner, *The Dynamic Element in the Church*, trans. W. J. O'Hara (New York: Herder and Herder, 1964), 129-141.

29. Meister Eckhart, "Woman, the Hour is Coming," "Like a Vase of Massive Gold," and "Saul Rose from the Ground," sermons in: *Meister Eckhart: Mystic and Philosopher*, trans. with commentary by Reiner Shürmann (Bloomington, Indiana: Indiana University Press, 1978), 55-130. I have not found a really good English word to translate Eckhart's rich and important word *Gelassenheit*. The German word as he uses it connotes at the same time detachment, tranquility, and being empowered from beyond oneself. Sometimes the word is translated "releasement," but this is hardly a standard English word.

V

THE GALILEAN VISION:
ADUMBRATIONS OF PERFECTION,
HUMAN AND DIVINE

Those of us who find in the present phase of Western history a twilight time, the "eclipse," or even the "death" of God, are positively eager to renew the lifegiving tradition of speech about the Eternal. "As the heart panteth after water, so panteth my soul after you, O God" (Ps 42:1). The attempt, in the 1960's, to develop a form of Godless Christianity, however intriguing, was far from satisfying. The recovery of speech about God, however, is not a matter of will; it is dependent upon a recovery of context. As Reinhold Niebuhr repeatedly warned, nothing is as irrelevant as an answer to a question not being asked. As long as the context of human living was defined as that of acting and valuing, on the one hand, and knowing, on the other, and as long as knowing was exclusively understood in terms of scientific mastery or of the will to power, there was no context in which speech about God could be meaningful. God is neither a mere arbitrarily posited value, i.e., a product of the will, nor the object of a scientific hypothesis. And we human beings, as lordlike subjects, seeking to master the world are closed to the Transcendent, have turned away from the proclamation of the Word as from an object falling from outer space.

Nevertheless, neither technological mastery nor the will to power is the *basic* form of life-experience. Whatever truth may be found through adherence to a method, more truth and more revelatory truth are found in free dialogue, for fellowship is more fundamental and ultimately more fruitful than domination. Dialogue projects and depends upon a shared horizon in which agreements can occur and differences be mediated. This horizon is akin to a universal environment, a mysterious ultimate context within which you and I and all of our neighbors and fellow creatures can "live, move, and have our being." It is not a horizon we shall ever entirely understand but serves as the light in which we can journey in our quest for understanding.

Christian theology is not the only language in which to speak of this universal horizon, but it offers *one way* to speak of it. Anselm urged that the very notion of God includes necessary existence. Hence, as we saw in the first chapter, to speak of a God that sometimes exists and sometimes does not, or may not, is to violate the depth-grammar appropriate to the subject matter of divine perfection. "God" names the reality or being who is the creator of "all things visible and invisible" (Nicea), the ground of all things actual and also those that are even so much as possible. God, then, by definition, is somehow a dimension of *every* conceivable state-of-affairs or of none at all. We must accordingly acknowledge a certain fit between the omnipresent and universal horizon within which all dialogue occurs, or at least tends, and talk of a God who is the invariant ground of all that is or could be. Speech about God correlates with this context.

What more, however, might Christians today want to say about God beyond that God is the silent, unobtrusive, encompassing abyss of mystery and ground of intelligibility, this incomprehensible but supportive environment within which we exist? At this point we pause, for is there not something within us that hesitates to say more for fear of saying less, and indeed fears that perhaps too much has already been said? Melanchton advised that we would do better to "adore the mysteries of the Godhead" than to attempt "to investigate them." Mystics from the East and West alike would agree with the Vedantist Sankara's confession that before God "all words recoil." Aristotle remarked that human beings are as little equipped to talk about God as are bats to discourse of the sun. If such counsel had its point in pre-modern history, it can hardly be less applicable in an age in which our traditions are in disarray, our culture "honeycombed with bewilderment and a profound sense of internal decay," and our language and mentality shaped more by problem-solving than by contemplation.[1] Confronted by things of which we cannot speak clearly, why not follow Wittgenstein's advice to remain silent? Why not point to the implied, encompassing horizon, name it God, and confess God's perfection to be as incomprehensible as it is awe-inspiring?

Such verbal asceticism *may* be the path of wisdom. We nonetheless hesitate to take it for this reason: if we are to distinguish God from sheer nothingness, we must say *something*, however inadequate. It is not enough to say that God is perfect, for perfection itself is liable to various understandings. Unless we are vigilant, unworthy understandings of perfection slip in, giving the unholiest of connotations to the name and concept of God. That, in fact, happened early in our tradition, with results from which we still suffer.

This corruption of the concept of perfection prompted Whitehead's eloquent condemnation:

> When the Western world accepted Christianity, Caesar conquered; and the received text of Western theology was edited by his lawyers. The code of Justinian and the theology of Justinian are two volumes expressing one movement of the human spirit. The brief Galilean vision of humility flickered throughout the ages, uncertainly. In the official formulation of the religion it assumed the trivial form of the mere attribution to the Jews that they cherished a misconception about their Messiah. But the deeper idolatry, of the fashioning of God in the image of the Egyptian, Persian, and Roman imperial rulers, was retained. The Church gave unto God the attributes which belonged exclusively to Caesar.[2]

The Galilean vision was corrupted in several ways.
First, in a *crude* political sense, Christianity has been co-
opted for imperialism. As Nietzsche showed, ecclesiastics
have exploited religion to establish and maintain power
over the laity. As both Marxists and Liberation theologians
are showing, upper classes use it to suppress lower classes.
Nations and races use it to exploit other nations and races.
(An African convert complained: "Once you had your Bible
and we had our land, but now we have your Bible and you
have our land.") We remember how wars of aggression
have been legitimated and sacralized by ceremonial prayers
and rhetoric. We have all heard "Onward Christian soldiers,
marching as to war, with the cross of Jesus, going on before." Second, the Galilean spirit was corrupted by the Cae-
sarean *conceptually*, a more subtle corruption. In the encounter between Christ and culture, Christ was allowed to
be subverted and shaped by culture, rather than allowed to
transform it.[3] The conceptual form was kept, in other
words, but the material content changed. Consider, for example, the messianic idea itself. Jesus' first followers found
it hard to revise their triumphalist notions of messiahship.
Jesus himself was unambiguous: "Whoever would be great
among you must be your servant, and whoever would be
first among you must be servant of all" (Mark 10:43-4).

An example more germane for our theme is the concept of God. The God of Golgotha has only sometimes
been allowed to convert the God of oriental despotism. Too
often the conversion has run the other way. This is what
Whitehead meant by saying that while our tradition high-
lighted humility and love, our systems of metaphysics have
all too often given pride of place to ideas of omnipotence,
immutability, self-sufficiency, etc—the ideals of Caesar, not
the virtues of Christ.

Nor, of course, was this *merely* a matter of metaphysics, something that might concern only philosophers.
As Calvin tells us in the first lines of the *Institutes*, knowledge of God and knowledge of self are virtually insepara-
ble:

> All our wisdom, insofar as it really deserves the
> name wisdom and is real and dependable, em-
> braces two aspects: the knowledge of God and
> our self-knowledge. These two have gone to-
> gether in various ways, and it is therefore not
> easy to say which stands in the prior place and
> produces the other out of itself.[4]

According to the Biblical religions, these two are so intimately related because we human beings are created in the
image of God, capable of reflecting God back to God and
thereby becoming a divine likeness in the world?[5] We are
called by Jesus to "be perfect as [God] is perfect."*It is of
the greatest consequence, therefore, how we conceive the
divine perfection.*

Jürgen Moltmann has recently explored ways in
which traditional monotheism has influenced different aspects of the concept of humanity in the history of the West.[6]
He points, for example, to the co-development of the notions of monotheism and monarchy. The idea that there was
"one God, one law, one world . . . [that] the world is dependent on God, although God is not within it," has gone hand-
in-hand with the belief that there should be "one king, one
will, one kingdom."[7] The political would thus mirror the
metaphysical order. Nor is the idea unique to Christendom.
Genghis Khan wrote to the Pope: "In heaven there is none
but the one God, on earth there is none but the one Lord
Genghis Khan, the son of God."[8]

Moltmann also shows the "echo" that traditional
monotheism has had in family life.[9] The *pater familias* has
felt called to represent the "omnipotent Father" in the
home. Hence, the traditional idea of a God who "deter-
mines everything, but is determined by nothing else" has
had consequences for the masculine self-image both in and
outside the context of the family. (There is, of course, a
Spanish word for that self-image, *machismo*.)

Moltmann also finds a correspondence between
classical monotheism, more especially the idea of the God
who dominates the world, and the idea of the soul called on
to dominate the body. As God stands vis-a-vis the world be-

low, so the soul is to stand vis-à-vis the body, determining it as much as possible, and determined by it as little as possible.[10] There is also the related but more general problem of the Western world's managerial and dominating orientation to nature at large. It is not only to the claims of our bodies that we are deaf, but also to the claims of the earth itself as well as to the claims of the fellow-creatures with whom we share it. We take the earth as grist for our mill; and we now speak readily of outer space as something we can and must "conquer."

These concerns inspire Moltmann to appropriate the trinitarian heritage of Christianity in a fresh way, thus reversing a tendency since Kant and Schleiermacher to dismiss trinitarian doctrine as inconsequential speculation.[11] In this, he is following the lead of Karl Barth and Karl Rahner, both of whom insist that the doctrine is connected in the closest way with the concrete revelatory event of Jesus Christ. In explicating this conviction, they affirm that God's being and God's action are identical. To use classical theological categories, they affirm the identity of the economic and immanent action and being of God.

This mode of theologizing has also been productively developed by Hans Urs von Balthasar and Eberhard Jüngel. Hans Urs von Balthasar, known for his dialectical response to Karl Rahner, agrees that the immanent and economic trinities are one; however he accuses Rahner of abstractness, arguing that the Incarnation must be centered on the cross.[12] The God who is revealed is precisely the self-giving God who exposes Himself to human rejection. This is the event that must be at the center of our trinitarian thinking. There is a cross "in the heart of God." Von Balthasar argues that the suffering of Jesus was not merely something that befell his human nature; in the cross we see the surrender of the Father as well as the Son.[13] In this double surrender von Balthasar finds both active and passive motifs. God takes the initiative in bridging the gulf created by sin, but in so doing God personally enters into the realm of powerlessness and death. In this "mystery of Holy Saturday," as von Balthasar calls it, we find the divine solidarity with the death of the sinner taken to the point where the internal unity (or *aseity*) of God is all but broken in the service of redeeming love.[14]

Jüngel and Moltmann share some of the same viewpoints. Jüngel's question, inspired by a deep encounter with modern atheism, is whether it is possible even so much as to think of God? Jüngel believes that modern atheism has shown us a contradiction in an all too common concept of God. More exactly, it has shown us a contradiction that exists between ourselves, as contingent and temporal beings, and a God who is in all respects necessary and timeless. Either God excludes humanity or humanity excludes God. If traditional theism inadvertently chooses the former option, then modern atheism self-consciously chooses the latter.[15]

Jüngel chooses neither. He challenges us to allow all *a priori* concepts of God, such as atemporality and impassibility, to be reformed by the concrete Jesus Christ-event. In this event, we see the idea of God's eternity become that of God's unique temporality. On the basis of the unity between the history of the Son and the life of the Father, we can affirm a saving solidarity between God and our history, rather than an ultimate conflict.[16]

I have mentioned some of Moltmann's politically and morally inspired criticisms of monotheism. In light of these concerns Moltmann has developed an understanding of God as a social reality. Many obstacles to belief, especially moral obstacles, could have been avoided, he argues, had the Christian tradition taken its original trinitarian insights as seriously as it did its belief in the one Lordship of God—as dominion in super power.[17] This is another instance in which inherited concepts, in this case those of "monarchical monotheism" have not been sufficiently transformed by concrete revelation. The tradition has so emphasized the oneness and unity of God that it has not been able to do full justice to the relatedness of God. We have already noted some of the ways in which human beings have been victimized by this proclivity for divine one-

ness and power. But the "first victim" of this tendency is
God, for sheer monotheism makes it difficult to see how
such an aloof Being *could* be related to life, which after all
involves manyness and movement.[18] God's sovereignty is
cut off from below, as it were.

This does not lead Moltmann to advocate simply
abandoning the notion of divine oneness. He proposes,
however, that instead of beginning with oneness and seeking relatedness, we start with divine relatedness and manyness and only *then* seek the divine unity. He also proposes
that we find a way of conceiving that unity other than turn-
ing to the traditional doctrine of "highest substance," for
the idea of substance has static connotations and is therefore anti-social and non-relational. The concept of unity
that we need is attained in true community.

True community is a model of manyness in oneness.
The individual integrity of each of the community's members is not compromised but preserved; yet the members
"are not there simply for themselves. They are there [rath-
er] in that they are there for one another. They are persons
in social relationship."[19] This Moltmann finds implicit in
the original trinitarian insight: the "Father can be called Father only in relationship with the Son; the Son can be called
Son only in relationship with the Father," and the Spirit exists in the love between Father and Son. Hegel saw the implications of this even better than most theologians when he
maintained that "personal being [*Personsein*] means to dis-
pose of oneself to others and to come in others to oneself."

Once we have taken seriously the reciprocity of the
divine persons, then we may begin to understand the real
unity of the Tri-une Deity. It is not the unity of static substance, but what John of Damascus called, eternal *perichoresis.*[20]

Greek theologians used the term *perichoresis* to ex-
plain that the whole, which the divine persons constitute, is
more than the sum of its constituent members, and yet is
not itself a fourth member of the whole. The word means
"to go/move around." Was there a connotation of playing or

dancing in the original? We easily imagine partners cir-
cling. There is a similarity between Moltmann's account of
the unity of the divine persons and Gadamer's analysis of
the function of the common horizon that makes dialogue
between humans possible, a horizon, we will recall, that has
a game-like quality. Dialogue is an experience where one
finds oneself in losing oneself, in being taken up into a
movement greater than oneself. One plays the game, yes,
but more importantly the game plays itself out, in, and
through us, its players.

　　Moltmann, in any case, sees an analogy between the
"unity that is sought by humans in their community, is anticipated . . .in their love toward one another, and is experienced in the ecstacy of joy . . ." and the unity of the divine
persons in mutual relationship.[21] In this sense and for this
reason, we must look for the *imago dei* (and human movement toward perfection) not only in individual persons, but
also in an authentic, loving community. Hence, the triune
God cannot plausibly be invoked to sacralize individualism,
isolationism, *machismo* ethics, etc. Perfection, both human
and divine, is more a self-giving and sharing affair than a
self-assertive one.

　　We have noted above the implications Moltmann
has seen between ideas of God and sexual identity. For
helping us all to see these and many other implications in
increasingly clear and arresting ways, we especially have
the feminist theologians to thank. They are providing an
original and increasingly influential contribution to social
and political ethics. They are also astutely and forcefully
calling our attention to the relationship between ethics and
ontology, that is, between ideas of human and divine perfection.

　　Mary Daly, for example, explains that her book *Beyond God the Father* is not just about one thing but many
inter-connected things. It is about the liberation of women
from oppressive social structures, liberation which is of a
piece with the liberation of the colored races from the
white, the poor from the rich, the Third World from the rest

of us, and nature from us all.[22] It is also about human liberation from false self-images, especially false sexual stereotypes of both femininity and masculinity, which foster "an alienation within the psyche" and prevent us from laying claim to parts of our own being which are projected entirely away from ourselves and onto the other."[23] This occurs when males deny all so-called "feminine" qualities in themselves—e.g., redundant emotions, receptivity, flexibility—and project them all onto women who are stereotyped as displaying *nothing but* emotions, etc. Or it may be assumed by both men and women that only men can be objective, aggressive, resolute, etc.[24] Further, the male stereotype is effectively sacralized in the widespread and age-old practice of thinking of the "Supreme Being," the *Summum Bonum,* as a Divine *Patriarch*, an almighty *Father* who rules his creation from above.[25]

Dorothy Sölle in an article, "Paternalistic Religion as Experienced by Woman," objects to the almighty Father idea from a different but related perspective. She finds that such an idea always seems to entail the belief that the authentic human relation to God is one of radical *obedience* and abject *submission*. Speaking not only as a theologian, but also as a survivor of the holocaust, Sölle finds the whole "Christian culture of obedience" and authoritarianism "offensive and dangerous."[26] The idea of obedience to authority should have lost "all its theological innocence," she says, by its association with Nazism. And she asks, "why do people worship a God whose supreme quality is power, whose interest lies in subjection?"[27]

In her first book, *A Chapter of Theology after the Death of God*, Sölle proposed that in place of the almighty Father, worship and devotion should centre on "the non-dominant, powerless Christ who has nothing to persuade and to save us but his love."[28] Now, however, she suggests that the Christian community learn to speak and think of God, not only as "father" and "son," but also as "mother" and "sister."[29] Mary Daly and Rosemary Ruether likewise voice this challenge to balance masculine images with feminine ones. The three independently suggest that there would be much merit in relativizing *all* parent images, through the discovery of images from the mystical tradition.[30] There we find a preference for understanding the human relationship to God as one of becoming "one with the whole," not of obedience to a parent, but of union, agreement, consent, at-one-ment, solidarity with the whole of Being.[31] The parent-image is a limited analogy, remarks Ruether, in danger of reinforcing patterns of "spiritual infantilism."[32] "The God(dess)," "who is both male and female, and neither . . . points us to an unrealized new humanity."[33] This God/dess is not the old God of God-world dualism; this God/dess is "the *Shalom*" of being itself. This God/dess is "the foundation" of both "our being and our new being."[34]

Contemporary thinking about God has taken the stand that Whitehead proposed: namely the retrieval of the "Galilean" model. Whether one speaks of the reciprocity of divine persons, or of feminine images of deity, or of the interaction of whole and parts, there is a lively quest, a groping, for more nearly social, dialogical notions of perfection. Whether inspired by a fresh retrieval of Biblical origins, or an encounter with modern atheism, or both, we are coming to see certain traditional ideas of God, perhaps not so much false as deficient, because they are onesided. This observation suggests a parallel between the earlier epistemological and the present metaphysical discussions. Both the dominant epistemology and traditional metaphysics have been guilty of dangerous, onesided over simplifications.

Traditional philosophy has tended to take the oversimplification as ultimate truth. Discreet data were interpreted in terms of a substance-accident scheme, suggested by everyday language; it was said that what we experience are substances qualified by universal traits. Descartes defined a substance as that which needs only itself in order to exist. Hume, who rejected both Descartes' doctrine of the mind and belief that our experiences mirror objective actualities, retained the belief that what we have are states of mind that are basically clear, distinct, isolated, and self-contained. The Humean analysis, while not totally fallacious, is far from being totally adequate, for it is an abstraction from a life-world that is dynamic, fluid, and interconnected, more organic than atomistic, more social than individualistic. While the atomistic abstraction obviously helps us get control of our environment, it is of limited worth as a description of the nature of things.

This abstraction or oversimplification, which was committed by classical empiricism, is matched by the similar oversimplifications of classical theism. Charles Hartshorne directs attention to two such oversimplifications. First, there has been the tendency to define God's perfection as "maximality of value such that nothing conceivably *could* be added to it, and from which therefore every form of self-enrichment, every aspect of process . . . is absent."[35] This means that God has been conceived as being in all respects aloof from the world of flux and finitude. Second, the tradition has tended to see the causality between God and the world as entirely asymmetrical: God moves everything, but nothing can move God, it has been thought, for God is in all respects immutable.[36] Now what is wrong in both cases, argues Hartshorne, is not what is affirmed but what is denied. There is, in the first instance, a sense in which God is unsurpassable: God's love is unflawed and boundless, hence unsurpassable by any other. However, as the world, which that love encompasses, can change, so also can the *content* of divine love. In the second instance, while it is true that God moves all; it is also true that as God exposes Godself to the weal and woe of others, others are permitted to affect God. God both acts and reacts, is both agent and patient; God both gives and receives.

Some of the theologians considered above would say the same about the masculine images of God. They express certain things that must be said of God, God's power, freedom, and the like. But these attributes are misleading when abstracted from more holistic images of God, images which are inclusive of feminine as well as masculine traits.

Taken by themselves, traditional theistic oversimplifications, which attributed to God male stereotypical attributes, have inadvertently conceived God's perfection in an antisocial way. Such a God, impassible, timeless, etc., would fit Descartes' definition of substance: "an existent thing which requires nothing but itself in order to exist" (*Principles of Philosophy*, Part II), as well as Aristotle's dictum that "[a substance] is not present in a subject" (*Metaphysics*). It is another question as to whether such a conception is adequate to render the religious insight, God is love, *Deus est caritas*.

I have argued then that both classical empiricism and traditional theism are one-sided. Both oversimplify for the sake of power, the will-to-power, to use Nietzsche's term. In the epistemological case, the oversimplification assists us in mastering our environment. In the metaphysical case, God is portrayed as mastering the world. Now if classical empiricism and traditional theism are parallel in these respects, another parallel seems obvious and important. Both are capable of being sublated into fuller, more social and dialogical accounts of things, in which mastering and controlling are only aspects and not the whole of the matter. Hermeneutical philosophy, we have seen, is completing classical empiricism (and the technological-scientific method built in accord with it) in the direction of a more dialogical orientation to reality. Here we have noticed the work of certain thinkers who seek to revise the concept of a God of power and self-sufficiency in the direction of a God of love, conceived as social-responsiveness. Both attempt to retrieve something like the Galilean notion of perfection.

This social notion of divine perfection is closer to the original Christian revelation than the more conventional notion. It is also more adequate to the philosophical challenges to belief in the modern age. So long as we persist in thinking of God, above all else, as omnipotent power, we will increasingly come to agree with Elie Wiesel and Richard Rubenstein in believing that God died at Auschwitz or with Antony Flew, who maintains that any instance of evil decisively counts against belief in God. All of them can charge God with either committing evil or failing to prevent an evil that God could have prevented. The very notion of omnipotence is dubious, however, in a social context, if it suggests that one agent has, or could have, a sheer monopoly of power. No doubt, the Caesarian notion of perfection still prompts some people to aspire to such a monopoly. The Galilean notion suggests, however, another idea of perfection, of a presence which "dwells upon the tender elements in the world, which slowly and in quietness operate by love . . . [a love that] neither rules, nor is unmoved."[37] Whatever else we may want to say about divine power, we may be learning never again to conceive it in abstraction from love, a love which respects the relative autonomy of the other, a love that will not overpower the other, but lives in fellowship with him or her. Of course, the theodicical problem is not so easily solved (if "problem" and "solved" are the right words). But as Bonhoeffer wrote from a Nazi prison, "Only a suffering God can help."[38]

Consider finally the challenge of self-assertive humanism. The Caesarian vision of the impassible, self-contained God, incapable of further enrichment, forces a cruel dilemma on humanity. We are forced, it seems, either to affirm a God for whom our world of flux, finitude, multiplicity, struggle, failure, growth, etc., are ultimately unreal, since it contributes nothing at all to the final and all-inclusive storehouse of perfection (i.e., God's). Or we must repudiate God, so as to affirm the earth, but at the price of depriving the earth of any final meaning. Both options lead to nihilism and thus to an untenable dilemma. Always *implicit* so long as God was conceived as the supreme omnipotent (in an unreconstructed sense) substance or subject, this dilemma has become *explicit* with humanity's "coming of age" in the modern period.

In the new thinking about God we sense a breakthrough in the making. As we learn to think dialogically of perfection, we find an emergent reciprocity between the world and God, time and eternity. God and the world need not be competitors. God's love for the world is such that God not only gives to the world, in the old sense, but also gives to the world the right to believe that the world can also give to God. Human beings, to be sure, can and do oppose God, but only by betraying their humanity, not by affirming it. Saint Irenaeus, outstripping the metaphysics of his day, put it this way: "the glory of the Creator is the creature fully alive."

On the imperial model, it was said that God was in the world. On the emerging social model, we can begin to see that the world is also in God. The sufferings and achievements of this world and life do not happen outside of God. God's solidarity with history is such that truly no one inflicts suffering on another without crucifying God, nor does any victim ever suffer alone. Neither does anyone ever give bread to the hungry neighbor or teach a child or write a poem or play a sonata or overcome injustice without adding to the joy in heaven.

The dominance of the managerial, technological way of being in the world, Buber observed, can shut out the light of heaven. I have not joined those who accuse that way of being as being unambiguously evil or entirely lamentable, but neither have I denied that there is darkness. I am glad to join those who continue to trust in the Light that shines even in darkness. As our civilization undergoes a major mutation, we need the effort of those few who are willing to work out, one by one, the changes necessary so that the Gospel of hope can be retrieved and reexpressed in our relatively new situation.[39] Some of the thinkers I have discussed are doing just that. These pages have no purpose other than to augment their labors.

NOTES

1. Margaret Lawrence, "My Final Hour," in *The Toronto Star* (January 17, 1987), Section M, 1.

2. A. N. Whitehead, *Process and Reality: An Essay in Cosmology* (New York: The Macmillan Company, 1929), 519.
3. H. R. Niebuhr, *Christ and Culture* (New York: Harper and Bros. Publishers, 1951).
4. John Calvin, *Institutes of the Christian Religion*, ed. J. T. McNeil, trans. by F. L. Battles (Philadelphia: The Westminster Press, 1960), Vol 1, Bk. 1, Ch. 1, 35.
5. Jürgen Moltmann, "God with a Human Face," in Elisabeth Moltmann-Wendell and Jürgen Moltmann, *Humanity in God* (New York: The Pilgrim Press, 1983), 91.
6. Ibid., 91.
7. Ibid., 92.
8. M. de Ferdinancly, *Tschingis Khan* (Hamburg: Rowohlt, 1958), 153; quoted in Moltmann, "Human Face," 92.
9. Moltmann, "Human Face," 92f.
10. Ibid ., 93f.
11. Moltmann, *The Trinity and the Kingdom of God* (London: SCM Press, Ltd., 1981).
12. Hans Urs von Balthasar, *The von Balthasar Reader,* ed. by Medard Kehl and Werner Löser, trans. by Robert J. Daly and Fred Lawrence (Edinburgh: T. and T. Clark, 1982), *passim.*
13. von Balthasar, *Reader*, 170-201.
14. Ibid., 150-153.
15. Eberhard Jüngel, *God as the Mystery of the World*, trans. Darrell L. Guder (Grand Rapids, Michigan: William B. Eerdmans, 1983), *passim.*
16. Jüngel, *Mystery, passim.*
17. Moltmann, "Human Face," 94.
18. Ibid., 94.
19. Ibid., 97.
20. Moltmann, *Trinity*, 174-176.
21. Moltmann, "Human Face," 98.
22. Mary Daly, *Beyond God the Father: Toward a Philosophy of Women's Liberation* (Boston: Beacon Press, 1973), 5.
23. Ibid., 10.
24. Ibid., 15.
25. Ibid., 18.
26. Dorothy Sölle, "Paternalistic Religion as Experienced by Women" in: *Concilium: Religion in the Eighties*, ed. by J. B. Metz and E. Schillebeeckx; English lang. ed. Marcus Lefébure (Edinburgh: T. and T. Clark, Ltd.; New York: The Seabury Press, 1981), 70-71.
27. Ibid., 70-71.
28. Ibid., 72.
29. Ibid., 73.

30. Sölle, "Paternalistic," 73; Rosemary Ruether, *Sexism and God-Talk: Toward a Feminist Theology* (Boston: Beacon Press, 1983), 68ff; Daly, "Beyond," 69-97 and 179-198.

31. Sölle, "Paternalistic," p. 73.

32. Ruether, *Sexism*, p. 68.

33. Ibid., 67.

34. Ibid., 70f.

35. Charles Hartshorne, "Whitehead's Idea of God" in: *The Philosophy of Whitehead*, ed. Paul Arthur Schilpp (New York: Tudor Publishing, 1941; second ed. 1951), 516.

36. Ibid., 516ff.

37. A. N. Whitehead, *Process and Reality: An Essay in Cosmology* (New York: The Macmillan Co., 1929; 5th ed. 1960), 520.

38. Dietrich Bonhoeffer, *Prisoner for God: Letters and Papers from Prison*, ed. Eberhard Bethge and trans. R. H. Fuller (New York: The Macmillan Co 1958), 164.

39. Bernard J. F. Lonergan, "Dimensions of Meaning" in *Collection*, ed. by F. E. Crowe (New York: Herder and Herder, 1967), 252-267.

INDEX OF NAMES

Lawrence, M., 101 (n.1)
Leister, D., xvi
Lewis, C.S., xi, xvii (n.1)
Locke, J., 66
Lonergan, B., 59, 66, 67, 69, 77, 84 (notes 2 and 6), 103 (n.39), 85
    (notes 15, 23, and 24)

Mach, E., 5
Malcolm, N., 13, 14, 19 (n.17)
Marx, K., xiii, 20, 23, 29, 36
Melanchton, P., 88
Meyer, B.F., xvi, xvii (n.5)
Mill, J.S., 5, 43, 44, 70
Milton, J., 72
Mitchell, B., 10, 11
Moltmann, J., 91-94, 102 (notes 5-7, 9-11, and 17-21), 93
Moore, G.E.,   66

Newman, J.H., 34
Newton, Sir I., 51, 52
Niebuhr, H.R., 59, 63 (n.74), 82, 86 (n.26), 87, 102 (n.3)
Nielsen, K., 9, 11
Nietzsche, F., xii, xiii, 20, 22, 23, 25-28, 30-36, 37 (n.37), 38 (notes 15-
    27), 39, 41, 57, 58, 61 (n.1), 77, 78, 80, 85 (notes 17 and 21), 90

Ogden, S.M., 85 (notes 16, 18, and 22)

Pailen, D., xv
Pailen, G., xv
Pannenberg, W., 85 (n.11)
Pascal, B., 36
Peters, T., 85 (n.11)
Phillips, D . Z., 18 (n.3)
Planck, M., 5
Plantinga, A., 18 (n.3)
Plato, 69, 77
Poincaré, 5
Polanyi, M., 65, 70, 84 (n.2)
Pope, A., 35
Popper, K., 7, 18 (n.5), 45

Quine, W., 48

Rahner, K., 82, 86 (notes 25 and 28), 92
Robertson, J., xvi
Robertson, J.E., xvi

INDEX OF SUBJECTS